Small
DREAM HOMES

President	Angela Santerini
Publisher	Dominic Foley
Editor	Darlene Fuhst
Writer	Jennifer Bacon
Graphic Artist	Bishana Shipp
Contributing Editors	Elen Erzhibova
	Molly A. McGuire
	Angela Mulder
	Laura Segers
Contributing Graphic Artists	Dana L. Gibson
	Joshua Thomas
	Diane Zwack
Contributing Writers	Paula Powers
	Claire Ulik
Illustrators	Architectural Art
	Allen Bennetts
	Anita Bice
	Rod Dent
	Greg Havens
	Holzhauer, Inc.
	Dave Jenkins
	Kurt Kauss
	Miles Milton
	Barry Nathan
Photographers	Walter Kirk
	Sean McGlincy
	Matthew Scott
	Laurence Taylor
	Happy Terrebone
	Doug Thompson
	Bryan Willy

A Designs Direct Publishing® Book

Printed by Toppan Printing Co., Hong Kong
First Printing, February 2008
10 9 8 7 6 5 4 3 2

ISBN softcover:

(10-digit) 1-932553-29-0
(13-digit) 978-1-932553-29-1

Table of Contents

Good things come

Small Dream Homes

Good things come in small packages, or so the saying goes. And in this collection of home plans that saying proves true once again. Like a timeless piece of jewelry, these small dream homes encompass luxury in even the smallest square footages. Details and amenities abound throughout the plans. While small might mean something different to everyone, luxury is a term no one can deny.

A dream home means different things to different people. For some it is the home they've always wanted and for others it is the beginning of a new life. Many young couples are itching to buy their first house and want a nice home with an affordable square footage, but are often unable to find a home that meets the budget and needs of a soon-to-be growing family. The same is true with empty nesters. Looking to downsize, empty nesters often don't want to give up the luxury they've come to appreciate in larger houses, but don't want to heat and cool a big, empty house. Enter *Small Dream Homes*. Separated in four categories to better help you find your perfect plan *Small Dream Homes* is the one place to find small yet luxurious homes for every budget.

in small packages . . .

Coffered ceilings, keeping rooms and well-appointed master baths are just some of the amenities found in these award-winning floor plans. Modest square footages and coastal or mountainous retreats become the ideal summer home or first-time buyer's refuge. If you're looking for luxury in a slightly bigger home, then look no further. *Small Dream Homes* also includes homes with more generous square footages that are perfect for those downsizing from a larger home.

Whatever your preference, *Small Dream Homes* perfectly captures the best floor plans for the square footage and effortlessly blends luxury with efficient layouts.

FRONT EXTERIOR: Stone and siding coupled with multiple gable peaks and an arched front porch create irresistible curb appeal.

MASTER BEDROOM: The spacious master bedroom is topped with a ceiling treatment for added drama, while the soft blue color creates a relaxing room for sleep.

DONALD A. GARDNER ARCHITECTS, INC.

Satchwell
SDHDG01-967

Graceful arches contrast with high gables for a stunning exterior on this Craftsman home. Windows with decorative transoms and several French doors flood the open floor plan with natural light.

Tray ceilings in the dining room and master bedroom as well as cathedral ceilings in the bedroom/study, great room, kitchen and breakfast area create architectural interest, along with visual space. Built-ins in the great room and additional room in the garage add convenient storage. While a screened porch allows for comfortable outdoor entertaining, a bonus room lies near two additional bedrooms and offers flexibility.

Positioned for privacy, the master suite features access to the screened porch, dual walk-in closets and a well-appointed bath, including a private privy, garden tub, double vanity and spacious shower.

GREAT ROOM: The stone fireplace, flanked by built-in cabinets, serves as a stunning focal point in the great room.

REAR ELEVATION

SCREENED PORCH: Sliding glass doors from the kitchen and great room provide a wall of windows as well as easy access to the rear screen porch.

DINING ROOM: A tray ceiling grants instant drama and elegance to the formal dining room.

KITCHEN: Stainless appliances and black countertops accent the vanilla colored cabinetry in the kitchen.

BAR: Instead of traditional built-in shelves, this homeowner chose to create a wet bar in the great room, and use clear cabinetry to display stylish glassware.

PRICING FOR
SDHDG01-967

SETS	PRICE
1	$665
5	$725
8	$775
VELLUM	$1090
CD	$1980

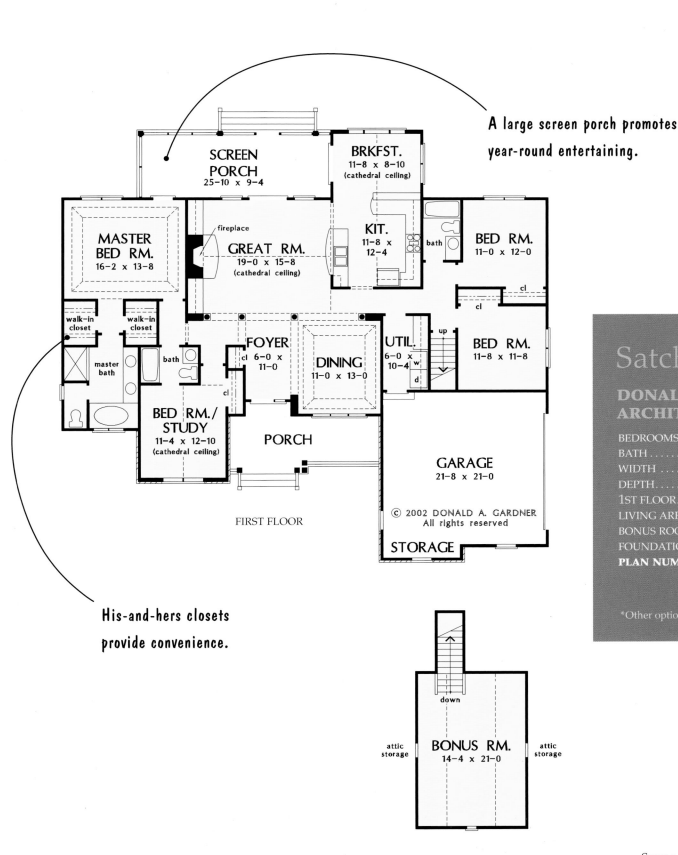

A large screen porch promotes
year-round entertaining.

His-and-hers closets
provide convenience.

FIRST FLOOR

© 2002 DONALD A. GARDNER
All rights reserved

Satchwell

DONALD A. GARDNER ARCHITECTS, INC.

BEDROOMS 4
BATH 3
WIDTH . . . . 64'10"
DEPTH . . . . 59'6"
1ST FLOOR . . . . 2097 sq ft
LIVING AREA . . . . 2097 sq ft
BONUS ROOM . . . . 352 sq ft
FOUNDATION . . . . CRAWL SPACE*
PLAN NUMBER **SDHDG01-967**

*Other options available. See page 175.

DINING ROOM: Looking over the rear porch and accented by a vaulted ceiling, the dining room is perfect for entertaining.

FAMILY ROOM: The vaulted family room features a striking fireplace that serves as an elegant focal point.

KITCHEN: The kitchen pass-thru and arched entryway enhance the open feel while creating a transition from the family room to the kitchen.

PRICING FOR
SDHFB01-3856

Sets	Price
1	$615
5	$665
8	$715
VELLUM	$810
CD	$1385

FRANK BETZ ASSOCIATES, INC.

BEDROOMS 3
BATH 2
WIDTH . . . . 50'4"
DEPTH. . . . . 49'0"
1ST FLOOR. . . . . 1406 sq ft
LIVING AREA . . . . 1406 sq ft
FOUNDATION. . . . . . . SLAB, CRAWL SPACE
OR BASEMENT
PLAN NUMBER. SDHFB01-3856

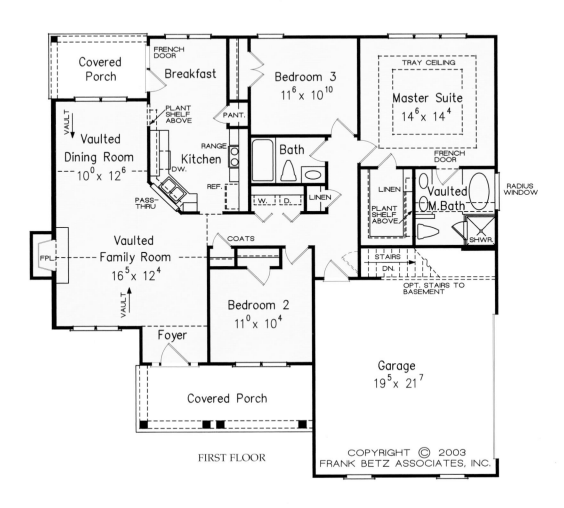

FIRST FLOOR

COPYRIGHT © 2003
FRANK BETZ ASSOCIATES, INC.

The two-story great room features windows on each level and a two-tiered fireplace that both draw the eye upward.

© The Sater Design Collection, Inc.

FRONT EXTERIOR: An elevated balcony entryway and varied rooflines greet those who pass by this charming coastal cottage.

BASEMENT: A full wet bar, sliding doors and white-trimmed windows give the finished basement its custom feel.

Aruba Bay
SDHDS01-6840

An elevated covered entry, cloud white trim and varied rooflines give lots of personality to this utterly charming coastal cottage. Multiple porches, a great room with fireplace and upper level bedrooms with a deck create a thoughtful, open floor plan that invites breezes, wide views and good friends.

Creative room placement in an unrestricted floor plan make *Aruba Bay* ultra-livable as a year-round or vacation home. Packed with functional and aesthetic details like a smart great room/dining room/kitchen design and large, sunny decks, the home invites fun, relaxation and memory making.

An oversized window and doors to one of the main level's three porches connect each space with the outdoors and welcome fresh air. Dinner guests can retire to either the great room's fireplace or enjoy the evening air, just steps away on the nearby porch.

The kitchen offers lots of storage and serving space with its deep, curved counter and a long wall of cabinetry culminating in a corner pantry. Open to the dining and great rooms, it's the home's center stage.

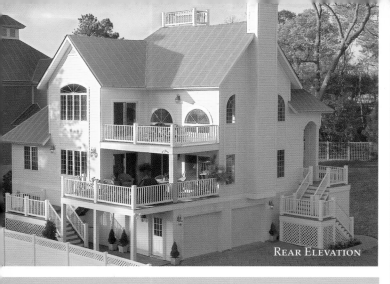

REAR ELEVATION

DINING ROOM: A large, airy dining room is just steps from the kitchen and great room. Enormous windows embrace the view while French doors provide access to the porch.

MASTER BEDROOM: The master suite is secluded to one side of the first floor and boasts an oversized bedroom with a private porch, plenty of storage and an opulent bath.

MASTER BATH: Amenities abound in this luxurious retreat complete with dual vanities, a whirlpool tub and separate walk-in shower.

GREAT ROOM: The fireplace welcomes intimate conversation despite the great room's epic proportions highlighted by the twenty-three foot ceiling.

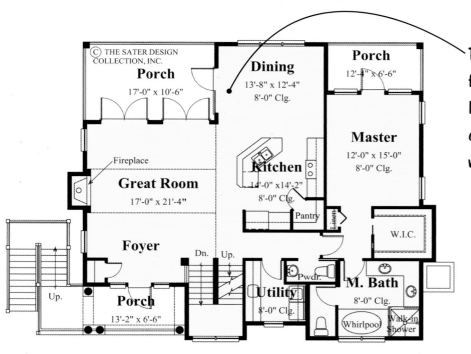

FIRST FLOOR

The first floor of this plan features both an open, interactive layout of the public areas and a quietly separated master retreat with a private porch.

PRICING FOR SDHDS01-6840

SETS	PRICE
1	N/A
6	$1132
8	N/A
VELLUM	$1132
CD	$2075

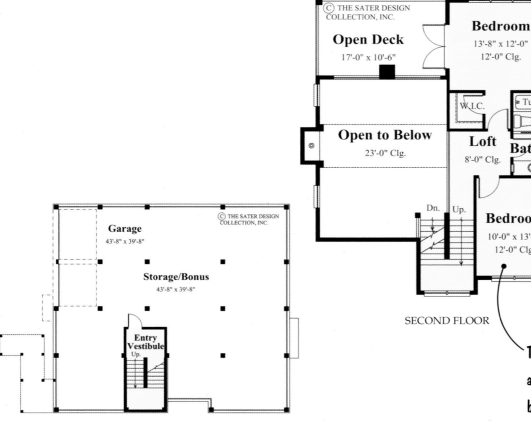

SECOND FLOOR

BASEMENT

Aruba Bay

THE SATER DESIGN COLLECTION, INC.

BEDROOMS 3
BATH 2-1/2
WIDTH . . . . 44'0"
DEPTH . . . . 40'0"
1ST FLOOR . . . . 1342 sq ft
2ND FLOOR . . . . 511 sq ft
LIVING AREA . . . . 1853 sq ft
BASEMENT ENTRY . . . 33 sq ft
FOUNDATION . . . . ISLAND BASEMENT
PLAN NUMBER **SDHDS01-6840**

Two bedrooms, one with a deck, and a shared bath are connected by a balcony hall that echoes the spaciousness of the first floor.

LIVING ROOM: This open and free flowing "casual zone" is designed for memorable days spent with friends. An extra-wide entry to the kitchen, paired with a generous pass-through, makes entertaining easy. Quality craftsmanship is evident in the built-in cabinetry and the beamed-vaulted ceiling of this airy space.

DINING ROOM: A unique ceiling treatment gives one-of-a-kind elegance to the formal dining room with coffered beams and bead board panel insets. Soft lighting streaming in through multi-paned windows creates a relaxing ambience, perfect for any meal.

KITCHEN: Located conveniently near the formal dining room, the kitchen features a center work island and plenty of counter space. Sliding glass walls open the area to the rear verandah and outdoor grille.

PRICING FOR
SDHDS01-6780

Sets	Price
1	N/A
6	$1731
8	N/A
VELLUM	$1731
CD	$3174

THE SATER DESIGN COLLECTION, INC.

BEDROOMS 3
BATH 3
WIDTH . . . . 72'0"
DEPTH . . . . 80'0"
1ST FLOOR . . . . 2885 sq ft
LIVING AREA . . . . 2885 sq ft
FOUNDATION . . . . SLAB
PLAN NUMBER **SDHDS01-6780**

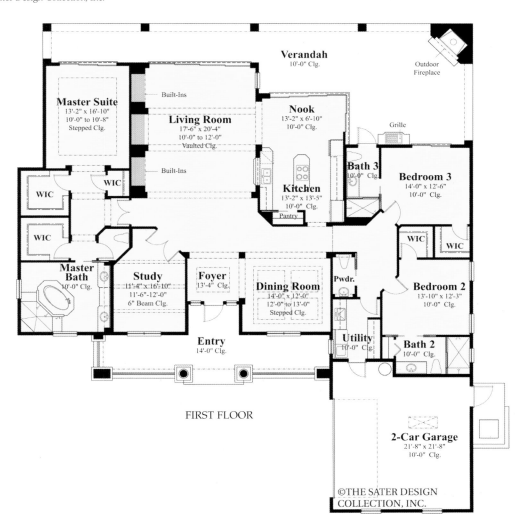

FIRST FLOOR

©THE SATER DESIGN COLLECTION, INC.

GARRELL ASSOCIATES, INC.

Melbourne
SDHGA01-05208

The *Melbourne* offers comfortable space with multiple living areas. An open floor plan gives a much larger feeling than the square footage suggests. The island kitchen opens to both the breakfast and angled keeping room; a perfect place to entertain family and friends. In traditional style, the two-story foyer is flanked by a formal living room and dining room. Completing the first floor is a bedroom and full bath. On the second floor, the master bedroom, boasting a luxury bath and spacious walk in closet, is conveniently separated from two additional bedrooms by the hallway. The two bedrooms share a bathroom with a dual sink vanity and private tub and toilet room.

FRONT EXTERIOR: A warm blend of shake and stacked stone gives this Craftsman façade distinctive curb appeal. A rocking chair front porch accented with twin columns provides a breath of fresh air and welcomes you into this lovely home.

BREAKFAST/GRAND ROOM: Open floor plan design brings main social rooms together, making it perfect for entertaining family and friends.

FAMILY ROOM: This cozy family room opens to the kitchen and breakfast area. A beautiful stacked stone fireplace flanked by windows adds a warm centerpiece for family and friends.

MASTER BEDROOM: A tray ceiling and premium molding detail give the master bedroom well deserved elegance. This private suite is complete with a dual sink vanity, separate shower and tub and an expansive walk in closet.

GRAND ROOM: The grand room is elegant and livable. Architectural details fill this room including a coffered ceiling, built-in book shelves and a fireplace with molding accents.

DINING ROOM: The finest dining can be had in this open formal dining room that fills with natural light.

KITCHEN: This gourmet kitchen with hardwood floors and stainless-steel appliances enjoys the convenience of an island sink and breakfast bar.

An angled family room enhances rear vistas and is a cozy complement to the kitchen and breakfast area.

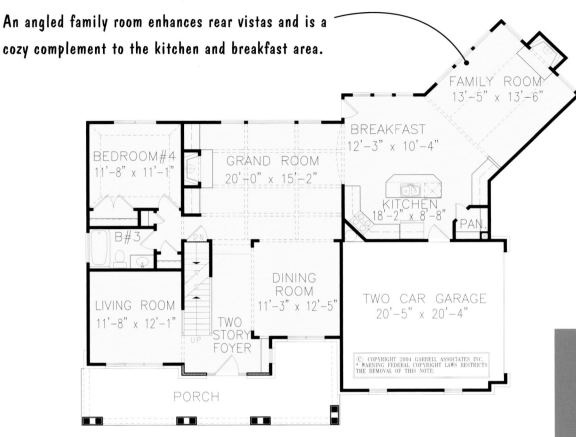

FIRST FLOOR

PRICING FOR
SDHGA01-05208

SETS	PRICE
1	N/A
5	$936
8	N/A
VELLUM	$1036
CD	$1886

Melbourne

GARRELL ASSOCIATES, INC.

BEDROOMS 4
BATH 3
WIDTH . . . . 62'4"
DEPTH . . . . 48'10"
1ST FLOOR . . . . 1537 sq ft
2ND FLOOR . . . . 1052 sq ft
LIVING AREA . . . . 2589 sq ft
BONUS ROOM . . . . 63 sq ft
FOUNDATION . . . . BASEMENT
PLAN NUMBER **SDHGA01-05208**

A convenient second floor feature is the laundry room.

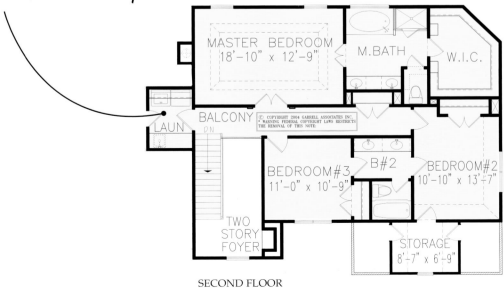

SECOND FLOOR

REAR ELEVATION

KITCHEN: Granite countertops, an undermount sink and center island make this kitchen both functional and beautiful.

GREAT ROOM: The great room includes many custom details: a fireplace, cathedral ceiling, clerestory window and French doors.

BREAKFAST ROOM: Modified from the original plan, the breakfast nook features a built-in buffet.

PRICING FOR
SDHDG01-780-D

Sets	Price
1	$710
5	$770
8	$820
VELLUM	$1155
CD	$2110

DONALD A. GARDNER ARCHITECTS, INC.

BEDROOMS 4
BATH 3-1/2
WIDTH . . . . 81'4"
DEPTH . . . . 68'8"
1ST FLOOR . . . . 1662 sq ft
2ND FLOOR . . . . 585 sq ft
LIVING AREA . . . . 2953 sq ft
BONUS ROOM . . . . 575 sq ft
FOUNDATION . . . . HILLSIDE
WALKOUT
PLAN NUMBER SDHDG01-780-D

SECOND FLOOR

BED RM.
11-8 x 13-0

great room below

bath

BED RM.
11-8 x 12-4

railing

foyer below

down

down

BONUS RM.
13-2 x 41-0

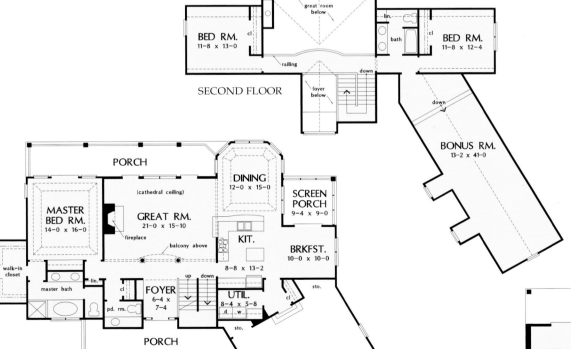

FIRST FLOOR

PORCH

MASTER BED RM.
14-0 x 16-0

GREAT RM.
21-0 x 15-10
(cathedral ceiling)

fireplace

balcony above

DINING
12-0 x 15-0

SCREEN PORCH
9-4 x 9-0

KIT.

BRKFST.
10-0 x 10-0

walk-in closet

master bath

lin.

FOYER
6-4 x 7-4

UTIL.
8-4 x 5-8

pd. rm.

d   w

up   down

sto.

sto.

PORCH

GARAGE
22-0 x 34-0

BASEMENT

PATIO

UNFINISHED STORAGE/ MECHANICAL
13-4 x 15-6

fireplace

FAMILY RM.
17-10 x 15-4

wet bar

BED RM./ STUDY
12-2 x 10-0

bath

sto.

up

© 2002 Frank Betz Associates, Inc.

FRONT EXTERIOR: The traditional exterior of the *Gastonia* is defined by brick and siding and an inviting front porch.

SITTING ROOM: The sitting room makes the master suite truly spectacular, however, this room can be converted into an additional bedroom if extra space is needed.

FRANK BETZ ASSOCIATES, INC.

Gastonia
SDHFB01-3271

Smaller homes don't have to lack upscale amenities! The *Gastonia* includes many special features often hard to find even in larger homes. The master suite has a comfortable sitting room, large enough for lounging furniture. However, if a fourth bedroom is a higher priority, this space can be easily converted to accommodate it. Each secondary bedroom features a walk-in closet. An island serves as the center point of the kitchen and helps with meal preparation. Decorative columns and an art niche on the main floor give the main floor extra flavor for decorating. A sink is designed into the laundry room; a practical and useful added feature.

KITCHEN/BREAKFAST: The spacious kitchen and breakfast room create a natural traffic flow into the great room.

GREAT ROOM: With views to the outdoors, the great room features an intimate sitting area beside built-in cabinetry.

MASTER SUITE: A tray ceiling in the master suite shows off style, while the wall of windows bathes the room with sunlight.

FRANK BETZ ASSOCIATES, INC.

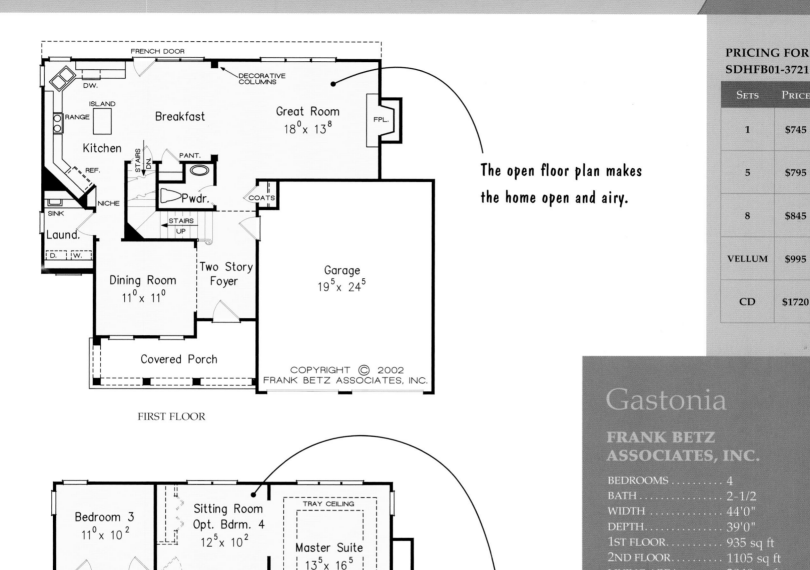

FIRST FLOOR

SECOND FLOOR

The open floor plan makes the home open and airy.

His-and-hers closets are an added treat.

PRICING FOR SDHFB01-3721

SETS	PRICE
1	$745
5	$795
8	$845
VELLUM	$995
CD	$1720

Gastonia

FRANK BETZ ASSOCIATES, INC.

BEDROOMS 4
BATH 2-1/2
WIDTH . . . . 44'0"
DEPTH . . . . 39'0"
1ST FLOOR . . . . 935 sq ft
2ND FLOOR . . . . 1105 sq ft
LIVING AREA . . . . 2040 sq ft
FOUNDATION . . . . SLAB, CRAWL SPACE OR BASEMENT
PLAN NUMBER **SDHFB01-3721**

Side Porch: Enjoying alfresco meals or watching sunsets is a breeze on the side porch.

Kitchen/Dining/Great Room: The kitchen, dining and great room are all open to one another, allowing conversation to flow freely from room to room.

Master Bedroom: Opening onto a rear deck, the master bedroom welcomes the outdoors inside.

Kitchen: Stainless-steel appliances and black countertops complement the rustic-looking cabinetry in the kitchen.

Riva Ridge

PRICING FOR SDHDG01-5013

Sets	Price
1	$956
5	$1040
8	$1110
VELLUM	$1432
CD	$2864

DONALD A. GARDNER ARCHITECTS, INC.

BEDROOMS 4
BATH 4
WIDTH .... 60'6"
DEPTH.............. 41'7"
1ST FLOOR.......... 1428 sq ft
BASEMENT .... 835 sq ft
LIVING AREA .... 2263 sq ft
FOUNDATION....... HILLSIDE WALKOUT
PLAN NUMBER..... SDHAL01-5013

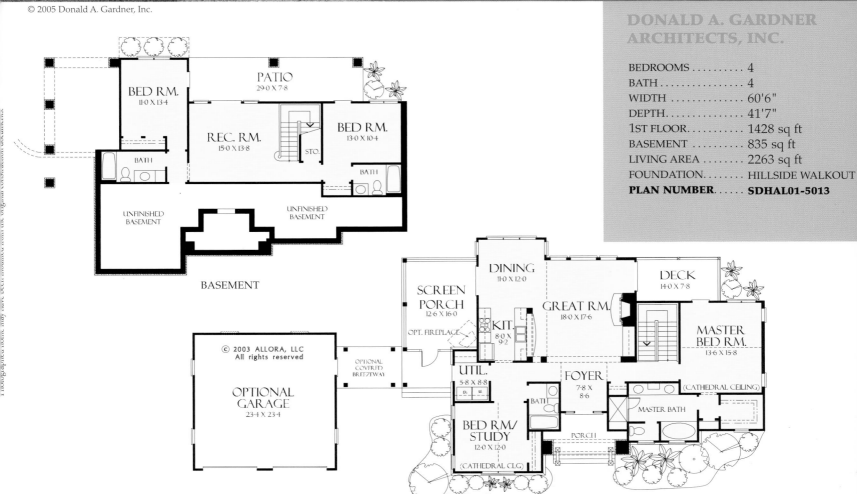

BASEMENT

FIRST FLOOR

THE SATER DESIGN COLLECTION, INC.

Kinsey
SDHDS01-6756

Warm and intimate, the *Kinsey* delights with perfectly thought out family living spaces, elegant and functional interior details, a Mediterranean façade and portico entry.

The interior is filled with unique architectural details that provide easy living amidst elegant appointments. The kitchen's center island and sophisticated appliances please the most discerning cook, while Tuscan details add a subtle Mediterranean spark to the room. Adjacent is a bayed eating nook and leisure room with open access to the lanai. A built-in entertainment center, dry bar and a server niche guarantee easy entertaining. The dining and formal living room offer an opulent setting for entertaining. A deep coffer embraces fine art and furniture in the dining room, while built-in bookshelves add a special touch to the living room. Stepped ceilings soar over both rooms, and disappearing glass doors open the living room to the lanai.

FRONT EXTERIOR: This special home uniquely blends a triple arched entry with stucco and banded detail to give it a Mediterranean feel.

KITCHEN: A state-of-the-art kitchen is open to a dining nook and leisure room and also features an eating bar.

LIVING ROOM: Soft lighting and fresh breezes invited by retreating the glass walls infuse the formal living room with a serene, al fresco ambience.

LEISURE ROOM: The leisure room flows seamlessly into the gourmet kitchen, providing a delightful environment for festive entertaining as well as cozy family movie nights.

MASTER BEDROOM: The intimate master suite comprises an entire wing of the home and boasts a bay-window bedroom, walk-in closet with adjacent dressing area, and a corner tub facing a private garden.

DINING ROOM: Repeating arches and a striking stepped ceiling make even everyday meals enjoyed in this room feel like a special occasion.

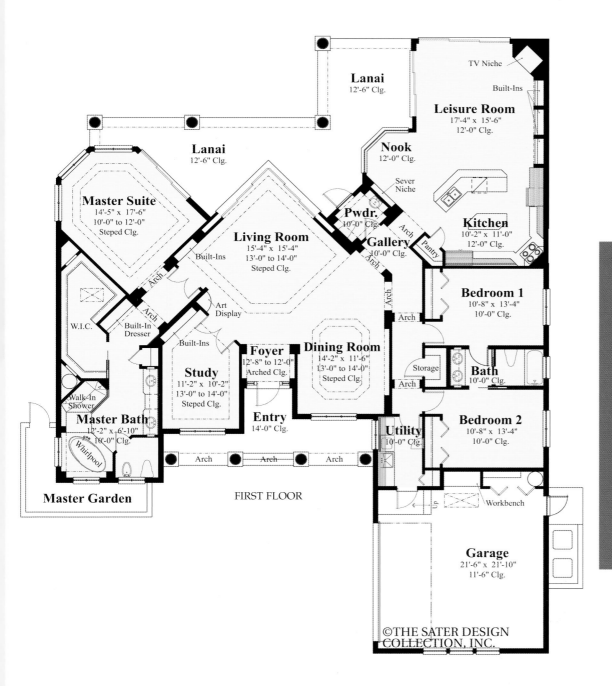

Lanai 12'-6" Clg.

TV Niche

Built-Ins

Leisure Room 17'-4" x 15'-6" 12'-0" Clg.

Lanai 12'-6" Clg.

Nook 12'-0" Clg.

Sever Niche

Master Suite 14'-5" x 17'-6" 10'-0" to 12'-0" Steped Clg.

Pwdr. 10'-0" Clg.

Living Room 15'-4" x 15'-4" 13'-0" to 14'-0" Steped Clg.

Kitchen 10'-2" x 11'-0" 12'-0" Clg.

Built-Ins

Gallery 10'-0" Clg.

Pantry

W.I.C.

Built-In Dresser

Arch

Arch

Art Display

Built-Ins

Bedroom 1 10'-8" x 13'-4" 10'-0" Clg.

Arch

Foyer 12'-8" to 12'-0" Arched Clg.

Dining Room 14'-2" x 11'-6" 13'-0" to 14'-0" Steped Clg.

Study 11'-2" x 10'-2" 13'-0" to 14'-0" Steped Clg.

Storage

Bath 10'-0" Clg.

Arch

Walk-In Shower

Master Bath 12'-2" x 6'-10" 10'-0" Clg.

Entry 14'-0" Clg.

Utility 10'-0" Clg.

Bedroom 2 10'-8" x 13'-4" 10'-0" Clg.

Whirlpool

Arch

Arch

Arch

Master Garden

FIRST FLOOR

Up

Workbench

Garage 21'-6" x 21'-10" 11'-6" Clg.

©THE SATER DESIGN COLLECTION, INC.

Kinsey

THE SATER DESIGN COLLECTION, INC.

BEDROOMS 3
BATH 2-1/2
WIDTH . . . . 65'0"
DEPTH . . . . 84'0"
1ST FLOOR . . . . 2907 sq ft
LIVING AREA . . . . 2907 sq ft
FOUNDATION . . . . SLAB
PLAN NUMBER SDHDS01-6756

REAR ELEVATION

BREAKFAST/KITCHEN: The very essence of entertaining is captured by the *Monroe*. The kitchen, breakfast area and family room form expansive open areas suitable for large gatherings.

SUNROOM: Paneled accents, built-in shelves and arched window treatments create a warm place for quiet time.

DINING ROOM: A detailed ceiling gives this stunning formal dining room an elegant flair.

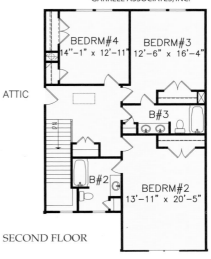

Monroe

PRICING FOR SDHGA01-04228

Sets	Price
1	N/A
5	$1395
8	N/A
VELLUM	$1495
CD	$2345

GARRELL ASSOCIATES, INC.

BEDROOMS	4
BATH	3-1/2
WIDTH	62'0"
DEPTH	78'8"
1ST FLOOR	2175 sq ft
2ND FLOOR	991 sq ft
LIVING AREA	3166 sq ft
FOUNDATION	SLAB
PLAN NUMBER	SDHGA01-04228

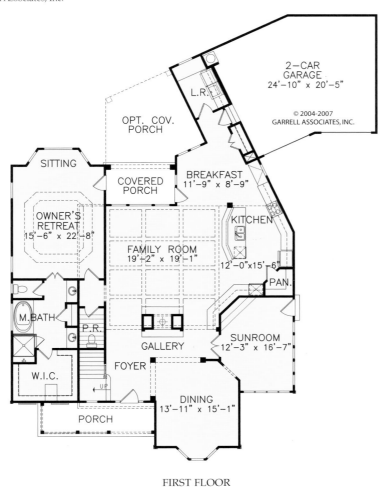

2-CAR GARAGE 24'-10" x 20'-5"

L.R.

OPT. COV. PORCH

COVERED PORCH

BREAKFAST 11'-9" x 8'-9"

KITCHEN

SITTING

OWNER'S RETREAT 15'-6" x 22'-8"

FAMILY ROOM 19'-2" x 19'-1"

12'-0"x15'-6"

PAN.

M.BATH

P.R.

GALLERY

SUNROOM 12'-3" x 16'-7"

W.I.C.

FOYER

UP

PORCH

DINING 13'-11" x 15'-1"

FIRST FLOOR

ATTIC

BEDRM#4 14'-1" x 12'-11"

BEDRM#3 12'-6" x 16'-4"

B#3

B#2

BEDRM#2 13'-11" x 20'-5"

SECOND FLOOR

FRONT EXTERIOR: Traditions of the Arts-and-Crafts movement meet modern living in this distinctive design featuring a welcoming pergola, period-inspired windows and a stylish roof overhang.

HEARTH ROOM: The linear custom furniture layout in the family room directs your eye to its lake view. The simple extended headers complement the furnishings without drawing too much attention.

VISBEEN ASSOCIATES, INC.

Amblewood
SDHVA01-9004

Arts-and-Crafts style meets the modern world in this well-planned home designed for a small, narrow lot. Low pitched roofs, interesting overhangs and natural tones on the exterior blend with the environment and can be carried into the interior, which includes an convenient open floor plan. A large kitchen serves as the central gathering area, with family room, living and dining room, porches and raised patio nearby. The upstairs features a large master suite, a guest bedroom and a bunkroom that sleeps six.

FOYER: The combination of the Arts-and-Crafts detailing with updated amenities puts the twist on the home.

REAR ELEVATION

KITCHEN: The combination of rich cherry cabinetry with the updated stainless-steel hardware and appliances make for a dynamic and functional kitchen. Ribbed glass and glazed tile are a counterpoint to the textured slate floors & polished stone countertops.

HALLWAY: The unique stair system offers dramatic views as you ascend. The open balcony offers visual interest from the main level while offering breathtaking views of the lake and conversation area.

HOME THEATER: Who needs Hollywood or the cineplex when you can enjoy movies from the comfort of your own theater and bar?

DINING/LIVING ROOM: The large, round dining table is centered in the home and offers views to the large patio and lake. The large, stone fireplace offers privacy from the neighboring home where it grounds the two-story living room. This stone wall is an example of balancing strong architecture with the clean lines throughout the home.

VISBEEN ASSOCIATES, INC.

Only 46' wide—perfect for narrow lots!

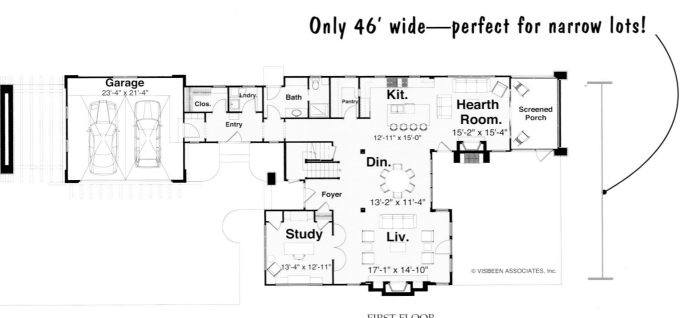

FIRST FLOOR

Bunk room sleeps six!

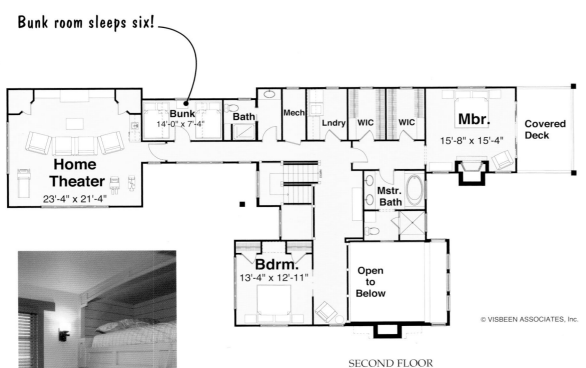

SECOND FLOOR

BUNK ROOM

PRICING FOR SDHVA01-9004

SETS	PRICE
1	N/A
5	N/A
8	N/A
VELLUM	$2095
CD	$1795

Amblewood

VISBEEN ASSOCIATES, INC.

BEDROOMS . . . . 2 + Bunkroom
BATH 3
WIDTH . . . . 46'0"
DEPTH . . . . 100'0"
1ST FLOOR . . . . 1961 sq ft
2ND FLOOR . . . . 1493 sq ft
LIVING AREA . . . . 3454 sq ft
FOUNDATION . . . . CRAWL SPACE
PLAN NUMBER SDHVA01-9004

KITCHEN: Golden cabinetry and granite countertops join together to create this breathtaking kitchen.

FAMILY ROOM: The main focus of this vaulted family room is the floor-to-ceiling stone fireplace.

MASTER BATH: Sharp colors mixed with natural materials reflect the homeowner's personality.

PRICING FOR SDHFB01-3894

Sets	Price
1	$745
5	$795
8	$845
VELLUM	$995
CD	$1720

FRANK BETZ ASSOCIATES, INC.

BEDROOMS 4
BATH 2-1/2
WIDTH . . . . 53'0"
DEPTH . . . . 55'0"
1ST FLOOR . . . . 1455 sq ft
2ND FLOOR . . . . 727 sq ft
LIVING AREA . . . . 2182 sq ft
FOUNDATION . . . . CRAWL SPACE, SLAB OR BASEMENT
PLAN NUMBER **SDHFB01-3894**

FIRST FLOOR

SECOND FLOOR

© 2001 Donald A. Gardner, Inc.

FRONT EXTERIOR: Multiple gable peaks combine with the towering portico and attractive garage doors to give this façade immediate curb appeal.

LOFT: The stunning loft overlooks the great room below and is the ideal kids play space or reading room.

Wicklow
SDHDG01-950

A unique mixture of stone, siding and windows create character in this Arts-N-Crafts design. A towering stone portico displays the grand entry into the home and showcases a French door flanked by sidelights and crowned with a transom.

An elegant, curved staircase highlights the grand two-story foyer and great room. Open to the great room, the dining room is the ideal entertaining space for formal meals. The dining room accesses the porch, providing guests scenery during mealtime. The kitchen is completely open to the large sunroom, and includes ample counter space, as well as a center island.

Upstairs, the loft/study area is ideal as a home office or child's playroom, and the bonus room can be used as a home theatre or rec room. Downstairs, the master suite is a true retreat. With a tray ceiling, the master bedroom invites relaxation.

GREAT ROOM: The gorgeous balcony draws the eye upward in this stunning great room.

KITCHEN: A large center island in the kitchen provides additional food preparation space.

MASTER BEDROOM: A tray ceiling in the master bedroom provides luxury and style.

GREAT ROOM: Exposed beams, built-ins and a two-story tall fireplace accent the impressive great room.

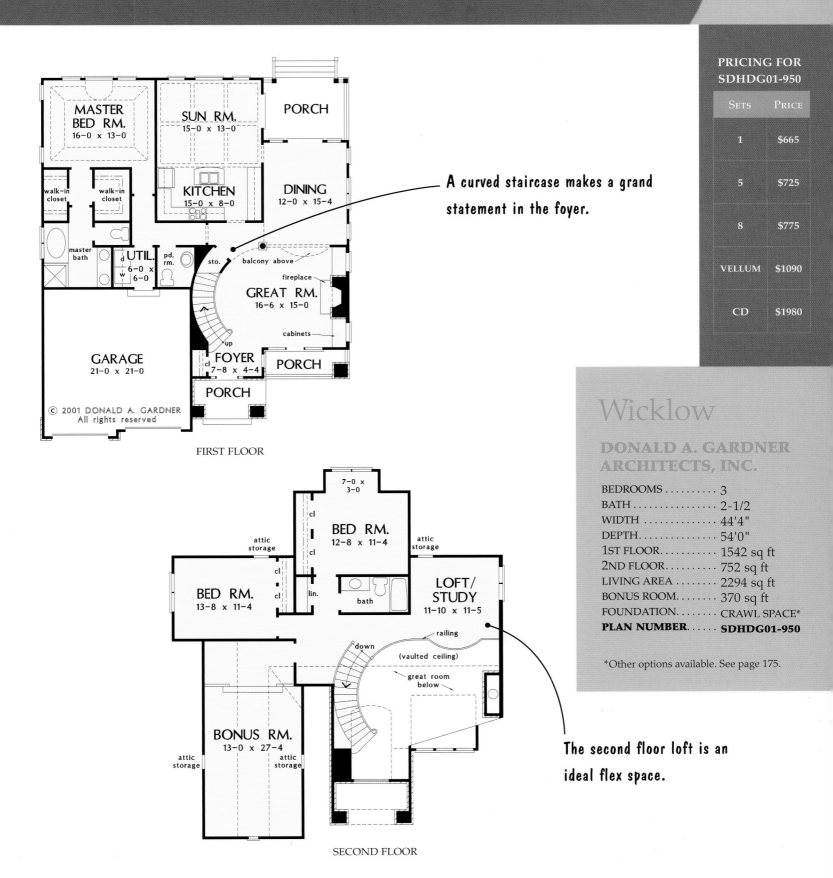

MASTER BED RM.
16-0 x 13-0

walk-in closet

walk-in closet

master bath

SUN RM.
15-0 x 13-0

KITCHEN
15-0 x 8-0

PORCH

DINING
12-0 x 15-4

UTIL.
6-0 x 6-0

pd. rm.

sto.

balcony above

fireplace

GREAT RM.
16-6 x 15-0

cabinets

GARAGE
21-0 x 21-0

up

cl

FOYER
7-8 x 4-4

PORCH

PORCH

ⓒ 2001 DONALD A. GARDNER
All rights reserved

FIRST FLOOR

A curved staircase makes a grand statement in the foyer.

PRICING FOR
SDHDG01-950

SETS	PRICE
1	$665
5	$725
8	$775
VELLUM	$1090
CD	$1980

Wicklow

DONALD A. GARDNER
ARCHITECTS, INC.

BEDROOMS 3
BATH 2-1/2
WIDTH . . . . 44'4"
DEPTH . . . . 54'0"
1ST FLOOR . . . . 1542 sq ft
2ND FLOOR . . . . 752 sq ft
LIVING AREA . . . . 2294 sq ft
BONUS ROOM . . . . 370 sq ft
FOUNDATION . . . . CRAWL SPACE*
PLAN NUMBER **SDHDG01-950**

*Other options available. See page 175.

7-0 x 3-0

cl

BED RM.
12-8 x 11-4

cl

attic storage

attic storage

BED RM.
13-8 x 11-4

cl

cl

lin.

bath

LOFT/ STUDY
11-10 x 11-5

down

railing

(vaulted ceiling)

great room below

BONUS RM.
13-0 x 27-4

attic storage

attic storage

SECOND FLOOR

The second floor loft is an ideal flex space.

BREAKFAST/KITCHEN: This very light and airy kitchen opens to an angled keeping room and breakfast area. Stairs lead to the second floor and a loft area above.

DINING ROOM: The formal dining room is crowned with the elegance of a tray ceiling. Hardwood floors and warm colors create a comfortable environment.

MASTER BEDROOM: This first-floor master suite provides a quiet retreat at the end of the day. A luxurious feeling is created by impressive molding detail and a tray ceiling.

Meadowmoore

PRICING FOR SDHGA01-05336

Sets	Price
1	N/A
5	$1495
8	N/A
VELLUM	$1595
CD	$2445

GARRELL ASSOCIATES, INC.

BEDROOMS	3
BATH	2-1/2
WIDTH	71'2"
DEPTH	67'6"
1ST FLOOR	2546 sq ft
2ND FLOOR	791 sq ft
LIVING AREA	3337 sq ft
BONUS ROOM	345 sq ft
FOUNDATION	SLAB OR BASEMENT
PLAN NUMBER	**SDHDG01-05336**

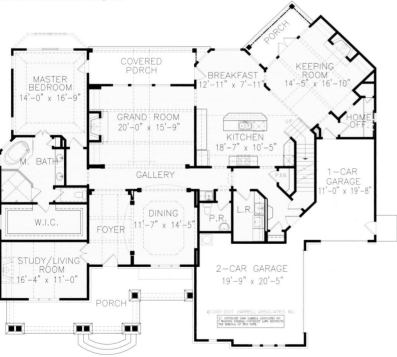

FIRST FLOOR

MASTER BEDROOM 14'-0" x 16'-9"
COVERED PORCH
PORCH
BREAKFAST 12'-11" x 7'-11"
KEEPING ROOM 14'-5" x 16'-10"
HOME OFF.
GRAND ROOM 20'-0" x 15'-9"
KITCHEN 18'-7" x 10'-5"
1-CAR GARAGE 11'-0" x 19'-8"
M. BATH
GALLERY
PAN
W.I.C.
DINING 11'-7" x 14'-5"
P.R.
L.R.
UP
FOYER
STUDY/LIVING ROOM 16'-4" x 11'-0"
2-CAR GARAGE 19'-9" x 20'-5"
PORCH

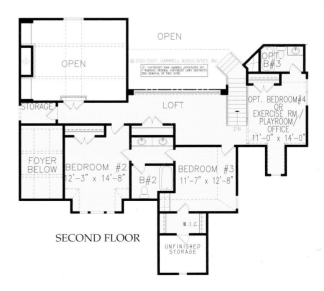

SECOND FLOOR

OPEN
OPEN
OPT. B#3
STORAGE
LOFT
OPT. BEDROOM#4 OR EXERCISE RM./ PLAYROOM/ OFFICE 11'-0" x 14'-0"
FOYER BELOW
BEDROOM #2 12'-3" x 14'-8"
B#2
BEDROOM #3 11'-7" x 12'-8"
W.I.C.
UNFINISHED STORAGE

FRANK BETZ ASSOCIATES, INC.

Ballard

SDHFB01-3633

FRONT EXTERIOR: A traditional exterior, the *Ballard* is complete with brick, cedar shake and a spacious front porch.

KEEPING ROOM: White cabinetry and molding create a beautiful contrast to the stone fireplace and crimson walls.

Abundant and transitional, the curb appeal of *Ballard* fully reflects its family with a tasteful representation of Traditional and Craftsman accents. Once inside, the two-story foyer foreshadows the openness to come. Showcasing the design flexibility, the two-story family room was modified to create additional square footage upstairs. However, it's the natural traffic flow that makes this home accommodating. Adjacent to the keeping room and breakfast nook, the kitchen proves it's the heart of the home with an angled center island. The desk creates a great homework or computer station, so parents can always be close by – even during meal preparation. Creating a homeowner's retreat, the master suite features a stylish tray ceiling, dual vanities, private toilet, separate shower and a tub.

FAMILY ROOM: With its coffered ceiling and classic fireplace, this famly room showcases refined comfort.

MASTER SUITE: This octagonal tray ceiling makes the master bedroom especially dreamy for homeowners.

KITCHEN: An angled kitchen countertop offers an abundance of room for more than one cook.

DINING ROOM: Molding, chair rails and an arched entryway complement the dining room's decorative ceiling.

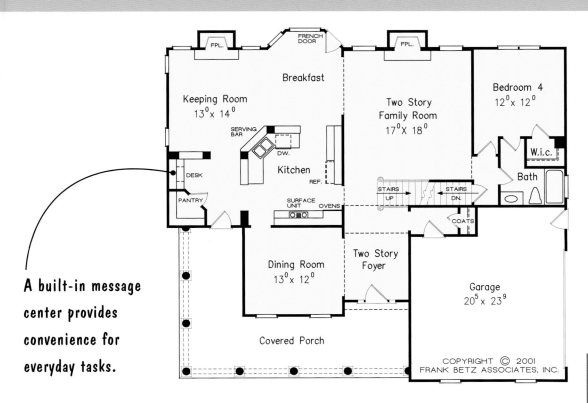

FIRST FLOOR

A built-in message center provides convenience for everyday tasks.

PRICING FOR
SDHFB01-3633

SETS	PRICE
1	$810
5	$860
8	$910
VELLUM	$1095
CD	$1895

SECOND FLOOR

This optional bonus room would make a great teen suite.

Ballard

FRANK BETZ ASSOCIATES, INC.

BEDROOMS 4
BATH 4
WIDTH . . . . 53'0"
DEPTH . . . . 48'6"
1ST FLOOR . . . . 1565 sq ft
2ND FLOOR . . . . 1194 sq ft
LIVING AREA . . . . 2759 sq ft
OPT. BONUS . . . . 280 sq ft
FOUNDATION . . . . CRAWL SPACE, SLAB
OR BASEMENT
PLAN NUMBER **SDHFB01-3633**

KITCHEN/DINING ROOM: A wraparound eating bar connects the great room to the kitchen. A center work island, built-in work desk and easy access to the dining room will please cooks of all levels.

GREAT ROOM: The substantial great room features a coffered ceiling, built-ins and open access to the kitchen and dining rooms. The great room and study share a double-sided fireplace and both rooms boast French-door access to the rear porch.

MASTER BATH: An indulgent walk-in shower and whirlpool soaking tub create a spa-like atmosphere in the master bath.

MASTER BEDROOM: A relaxing retreat, the master bedroom features a bay window, French doors opening to the back porch and a stylish tray ceiling.

© The Sater Design Collection, Inc.

SETS	PRICE
1	N/A
6	$1472
8	N/A
VELLUM	$1472
CD	$2699

THE SATER DESIGN COLLECTION, INC.

BEDROOMS	3
BATH	2
WIDTH	80'6"
DEPTH	66'6"
1ST FLOOR	2454 sq ft
LIVING AREA	2454 sq ft
BONUS ROOM	256 sq ft
FOUNDATION	CRAWL SPACE OR SLAB
PLAN NUMBER	SDHDS01-7065

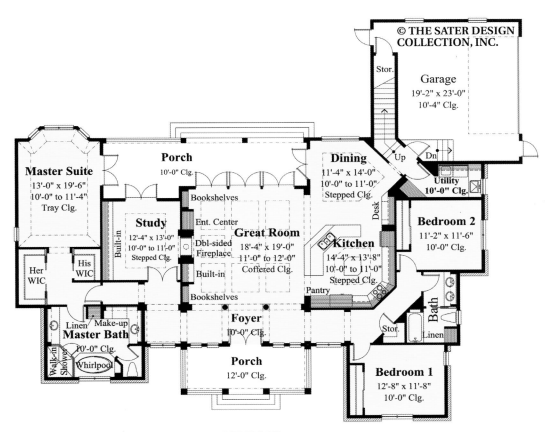

FIRST FLOOR

FRONT EXTERIOR: Modified from the original plan, stone replaces brick to give this Traditional a Craftsman façade.

GREAT ROOM: The great room has definition, yet is opened by a pass-thru and abundant windows.

DONALD A. GARDNER ARCHITECTS, INC.

Yankton
SDHDG01-933

This design takes a little of the Southeast and shares it with the rest of the regions through this stunning façade. Twin dormers separate two sets of matching gables, and the study's exterior and garage windows are accented with metal roofs.

The lavish foyer immediately spills into the open dining room. Columns are used to define the dining room, while a tray ceiling elegantly draws the eye upward. Gracefully flowing into the great room and adjacent kitchen, you'll want to serve all formal meals in this room. The kitchen is sizeable enough for more than one chef, while a pass-thru to the great room opens the entire space.

The master bath features a tray ceiling, ensuring ultimate indulgence via the garden tub and shower with built-in seat. The two walk-in closets and vaulted ceiling in the bedroom that complete the master suite.

DINING ROOM: Windows and transoms keep this dining room open and bright.

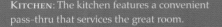

KITCHEN: The kitchen features a convenient pass-thru that services the great room.

GREAT ROOM: A clerestory window frames the sky and places it underneath the cathedral ceiling, creating volume.

BREAKFAST NOOK: The cozy breakfast nook looks out onto the rear porch and patio.

Every bedroom has a walk-in closet.

The master bedroom accesses a rear porch.

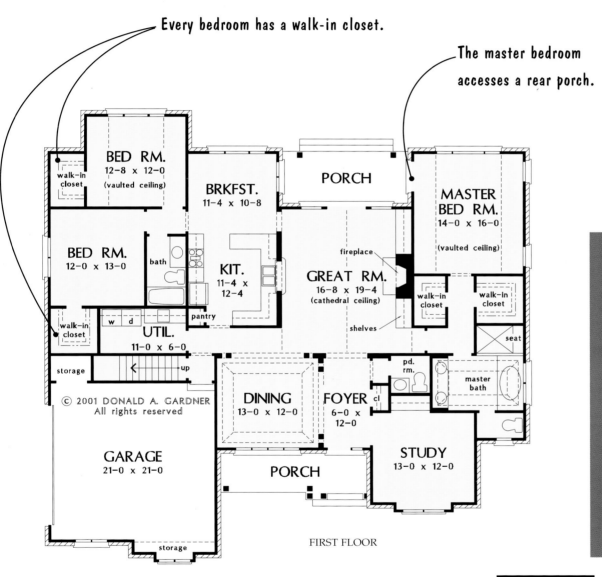

FIRST FLOOR

BED RM.
12-8 x 12-0
(vaulted ceiling)

walk-in closet

BED RM.
12-0 x 13-0

bath

walk-in closet

BRKFST.
11-4 x 10-8

KIT.
11-4 x 12-4

pantry

PORCH

MASTER BED RM.
14-0 x 16-0
(vaulted ceiling)

fireplace

GREAT RM.
16-8 x 19-4
(cathedral ceiling)

shelves

walk-in closet

walk-in closet

seat

w   d

UTIL.
11-0 x 6-0

storage

up

DINING
13-0 x 12-0

FOYER
6-0 x 12-0

cl

pd. rm.

master bath

GARAGE
21-0 x 21-0

PORCH

STUDY
13-0 x 12-0

storage

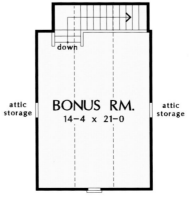

BONUS RM.
14-4 x 21-0

attic storage

attic storage

down

PRICING FOR SDHDG01-933

SETS	PRICE
1	$665
5	$725
8	$775
VELLUM	$1090
CD	$1980

Yankton

DONALD A. GARDNER ARCHITECTS, INC.

BEDROOMS	3
BATH	2-1/2
WIDTH	62'3"
DEPTH	60'6"
1ST FLOOR	2330 sq ft
LIVING AREA	2330 sq ft
BONUS ROOM	364 sq ft
FOUNDATION	CRAWL SPACE*
PLAN NUMBER	**SDHDG01-933**

*Other options available. See page 175.

KITCHEN: In this kitchen, the serving bar is a great place for quick meals, conversation and homework.

DINING ROOM: A triplet of windows with an overhead transom allows sunlight to flow throughout the formal dining room.

FAMILY ROOM: Polished describes this family room with its coffered ceiling, fireplace and built-in cabinetry.

MASTER BATH: Featuring a radius window, cathedral ceiling and a chandelier, this opulent master bath washes away everyday stress.

Stoney River

PRICING FOR SDHFB01-3866

SETS	PRICE
1	$870
5	$920
8	$970
VELLUM	$1190
CD	$2065

FRANK BETZ ASSOCIATES, INC.

BEDROOMS 3
BATH 3-1/2
WIDTH . . . . 65'4"
DEPTH . . . . 85'6"
1ST FLOOR . . . . 2876 sq ft
LIVING AREA . . . . 2876 sq ft
OPT. 2ND FLOOR . . . . . 393 sq ft
FOUNDATION . . . . CRAWL SPACE
OR BASEMENT
PLAN NUMBER **SDHFB01-3866**

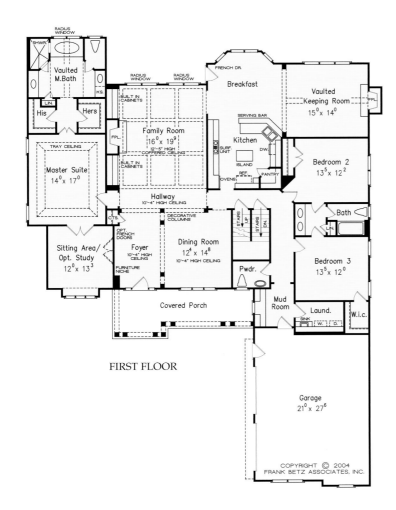

FIRST FLOOR

OPT. SECOND FLOOR

GARRELL ASSOCIATES, INC.

Nantahala
SDHGA01-06383

Promoting open living spaces, the *Nantahala* floor plan provides abundant places to enjoy calming views and elegantly blends the outdoors with indoor living spaces. From covered porches and multiple decks, to a large lodge and keeping room, this home embraces tranquil living.

Before you walk through the front door, take a minute to appreciate the beauty in the natural-looking exterior. A true mountain Craftsman façade, this home features ornately carved gable peaks, a sprawling rooftop with various pitches and a decorative single dormer. The covered porch provides a dry place to enjoy Mother Nature, while dramatic wooden columns punctuate the exterior.

FRONT EXTERIOR: A Craftsman-style façade of shake and stone, blend in with the natural surroundings of the *Nantahala*. Columns of rough sawn beams and stacked stone form the perfect entry to charming covered porch.

REAR DECK: A wrapping rear deck and covered porch maximize the panoramic views and are perfect for outdoor living and entertaining. A special feature is an outdoor fireplace for those chilly nights.

LODGE ROOM: The giant arched wall of windows provides a stunning way to enjoy rear views and natural sunlight.

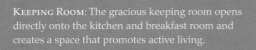
REAR ELEVATION

KEEPING ROOM: The gracious keeping room opens directly onto the kitchen and breakfast room and creates a space that promotes active living.

MASTER SUITE: Quiet time can be spent in the privacy of this elegant master bathroom.

KITCHEN: This gourmet kitchen features architectural details like no other from hardwood floors and custom cabinetry to a massive stacked stone accent over the stove. A landscape scene of tiles over the stove gives a perfect illusion of looking outdoors.

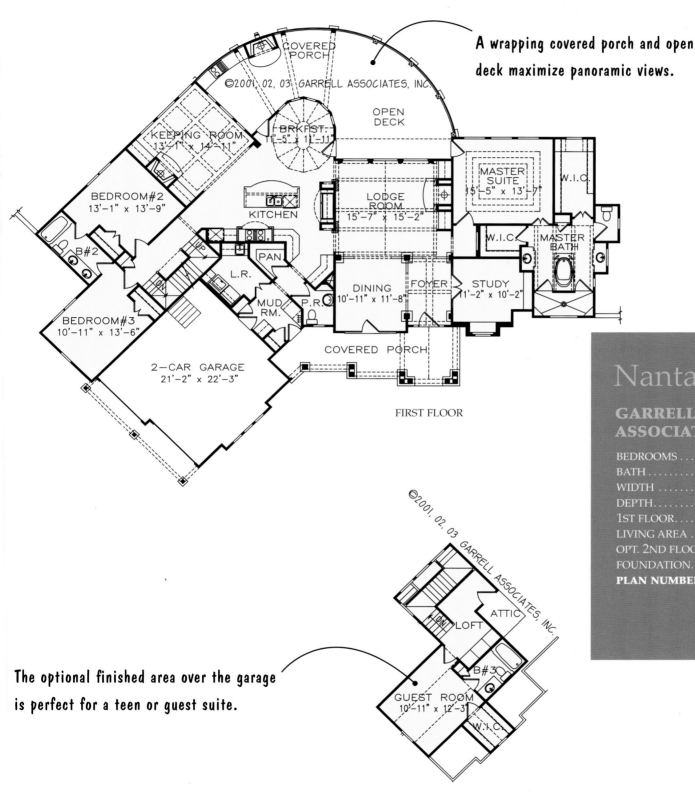

A wrapping covered porch and open deck maximize panoramic views.

©2001, 02, 03 GARRELL ASSOCIATES, INC.

COVERED PORCH

OPEN DECK

KEEPING ROOM
13'-1" x 14'-11"

BRKFST.
11'-5" x 11'-11"

BEDROOM#2
13'-1" x 13'-9"

KITCHEN

LODGE ROOM
15'-7" x 15'-2"

MASTER SUITE
15'-5" x 13'-7"

W.I.C.

B#2

W.I.C.

MASTER BATH

PAN

L.R.

BEDROOM#3
10'-11" x 13'-6"

MUD RM.

P.R.

DINING
10'-11" x 11'-8"

FOYER

STUDY
11'-2" x 10'-2"

2—CAR GARAGE
21'-2" x 22'-3"

COVERED PORCH

FIRST FLOOR

©2001, 02, 03 GARRELL ASSOCIATES, INC.

The optional finished area over the garage is perfect for a teen or guest suite.

LOFT

ATTIC

B#3

GUEST ROOM
10'-11" x 12'-3"

W.I.C.

OPT. SECOND FLOOR

PRICING FOR SDHGA01-06383

SETS	PRICE
1	N/A
5	$2295
8	N/A
VELLUM	$2495
CD	$3345

Nantahala

GARRELL ASSOCIATES, INC.

BEDROOMS 3
BATH 2-1/2
WIDTH . . . . 90'6"
DEPTH . . . . 73'4"
1ST FLOOR . . . . 2611 sq ft
LIVING AREA . . . . 2611 sq ft
OPT. 2ND FLOOR . . . . . 334 sq ft
FOUNDATION . . . . BASEMENT
PLAN NUMBER **SDHGA01-06383**

LIVING ROOM: This area just off the kitchen showcases a beautiful fireplace with cozy benches at its side and bookshelves overhead. The same earthy palette that colors the rest of the house adorns the fireplace in shimmery sandstones, colorful slate and metallic tiles.

KITCHEN: Arched ceilings, sky-colored walls, and outdoor vistas lend tranquility to what is quite often the busiest room of the home, while curved windows serve up a hearty portion of nature.

PLAYHOUSE: Tucked away in a corner at the foot of the stairs hides every little one's dream…a playhouse built right into the lower level of the home. It's the perfect place to escape while remaining in earshot of mom and dad.

PRICING FOR SDHVA01-9012

SETS	PRICE
1	N/A
5	N/A
8	N/A
VELLUM	$2095
CD	$1795

© 2003 Visbeen Associates, Inc.

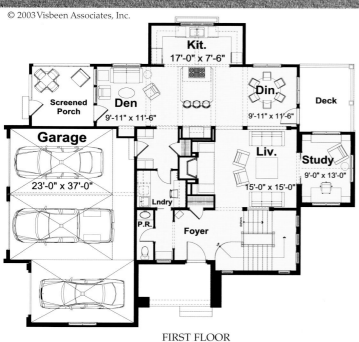

FIRST FLOOR

VISBEEN ASSOCIATES, INC.

BEDROOMS 5
BATH 3-1/2
WIDTH . . . . 64'0"
DEPTH . . . . 50'0"
1ST FLOOR . . . . 1564 sq ft
2ND FLOOR . . . . 1639 sq ft
LIVING AREA . . . . 4354 sq ft
OPT. BASEMENT . . . . . 1151 sq ft
FOUNDATION . . . . BASEMENT
PLAN NUMBER **SDHVA01-9012**

SECOND FLOOR

OPT. BASEMENT

© The Sater Design Collection, Inc.

FRONT EXTERIOR: Architectural detailing, including numerous arched window profiles, dormer accents and a corbel-enhanced, galvanized tin roof supports the cohesive design of this Tidewater-inspired cottage.

GREAT ROOM: The great room, with its soaring ceiling and parallel window configurations, is a warm and inviting space.

Carmel Bay
SDHDS01-6810

A high-pitched roof, plentiful windows and a sun-drenched porch come together to create a Tidewater-inspired cottage that is inviting…and stunning. Inside, a welcoming foyer exposes a charming arrangement of casual rooms. French doors lead to a quiet study, which features a wall of built-in shelves and panoramic views from the arched window. Across the foyer, a succession of arched openings and pass-throughs accentuate the effortless transition between the skillfully designed kitchen, great room and dining area. The open floor plan affords sweeping views of the outdoors through a multitude of windows and doors that open to the expansive covered porch.

Away from the public areas, a guest bedroom features French doors to the back porch and offers a quiet place to relax. Upstairs, a balcony hall showcases the living area below and connects the master retreat and second guest bedroom. In the master suite, French doors open up onto the exterior deck, inviting the outdoors inside.

GREAT ROOM: Matching custom-designed built-ins border each side of the fireplace that anchors the large room.

REAR ELEVATION

KITCHEN: Arched openings and pass-throughs accentuate the effortless transition between the kitchen, great room and dining area. The open floor plan affords sweeping views of the outdoors through a multitude of windows and doors that open to the porch.

MASTER SUITE: Tucked away from the main living spaces, the master suite features a vaulted ceiling, spacious bath and a private sitting room that accesses the upper deck.

DINING ROOM: Easily accessible from both the kitchen and great room, the dining room opens directly onto the home's expansive wraparound porch.

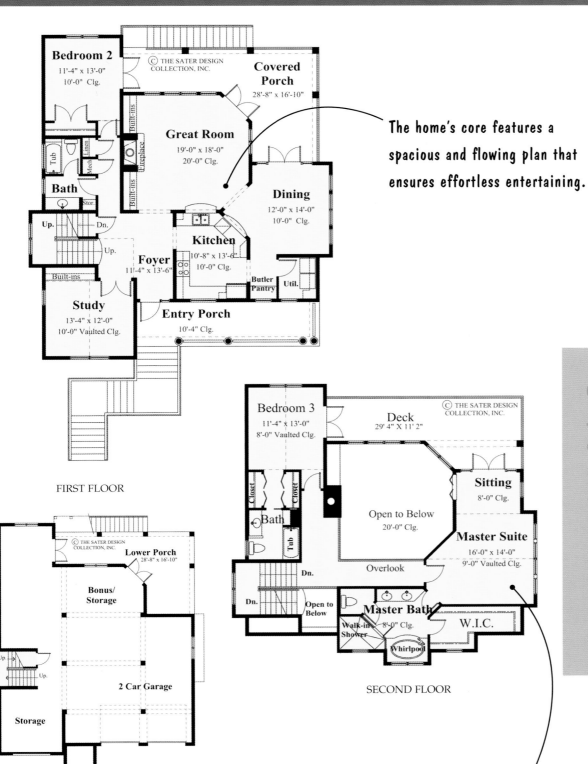

FIRST FLOOR

BASEMENT

SECOND FLOOR

The home's core features a spacious and flowing plan that ensures effortless entertaining.

Tucked away on the second floor, the expansive master suite offers large windows, its own sitting area and French doors that open to the upper deck.

PRICING FOR SDHDS01-6810

SETS	PRICE
1	N/A
6	$1508
8	N/A
VELLUM	$1508
CD	$2764

Carmel Bay

THE SATER DESIGN COLLECTION, INC.

BEDROOMS	4
BATH	3
WIDTH	46'0"
DEPTH	51'0"
1ST FLOOR	1542 sq ft
2ND FLOOR	971 sq ft
LIVING AREA	2513 sq ft
FOUNDATION	ISLAND BASEMENT
PLAN NUMBER	SDHDS01-6810

MASTER BEDROOM: A tray ceiling in the master bedroom grants striking architectural interest, while several windows bathe the room with sunlight.

GREAT ROOM: Natural light illuminates the great room, while a vaulted ceiling draws the eye upward.

DINING ROOM: Wainscoting, transoms and a tray ceiling create a formal impression in the dining room.

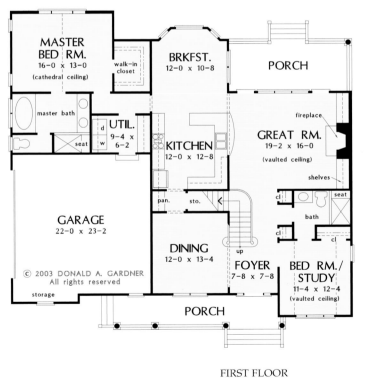

Derbyville

PRICING FOR SDHDG01-1032

SETS	PRICE
1	$665
5	$725
8	$775
VELLUM	$1090
CD	$1980

© 2003 Donald A. Gardner, Inc.

DONALD A. GARDNER ARCHITECTS, INC.

BEDROOMS 4
BATH 3
WIDTH . . . . 54'8"
DEPTH . . . . 53'2"
1ST FLOOR . . . . 1778 sq ft
2ND FLOOR . . . . 498 sq ft
LIVING AREA . . . . 2276 sq ft
BONUS ROOM . . . . 315 sq ft
FOUNDATION . . . . CRAWL SPACE*
PLAN NUMBER SDHDG01-1032

*Other options available. See page 175.

MASTER BED RM.
16-0 x 13-0
(cathedral ceiling)

walk-in closet

master bath

seat

UTIL.
9-4 x 6-2

BRKFST.
12-0 x 10-8

PORCH

KITCHEN
12-0 x 12-8

GREAT RM.
19-2 x 16-0
(vaulted ceiling)

fireplace

shelves

pan.

sto.

cl

seat

bath

cl

cl

GARAGE
22-0 x 23-2

© 2003 DONALD A. GARDNER
All rights reserved

storage

DINING
12-0 x 13-4

FOYER
7-8 x 7-8

up

BED RM./ STUDY
11-4 x 12-4
(vaulted ceiling)

PORCH

FIRST FLOOR

BED RM.
12-0 x 11-8

attic storage

7-2 x 7-4

BONUS RM.
13-2 x 18-0

attic storage

cl

lin.

bath

down

cl

great room below

BED RM.
12-0 x 11-0

foyer below

SECOND FLOOR

FRONT EXTERIOR: This Old-World elevation, with stone and brick, is a welcome addition to any neighborhood.

SCREENED PORCH: The homeowners of this magnificent home chose to add a screened porch to the back, allowing for an extension of the home as well as a retreat.

FRANK BETZ ASSOCIATES, INC.

Greenlaw
SDHFB01-3559

Stately brick, stone accents and a turret embellished with radius windows collectively assemble a distinguished façade on the *Greenlaw* design. A vaulted keeping room, breakfast area, kitchen and covered porch come together to create a comfortable core of the home where family and company will likely gather most frequently. The home office on the main level can be effortlessly converted into a nursery with easy access from the master suite. A loft upstairs makes a great lounging spot for the kids. Flexible space has been incorporated upstairs, as well, with an optional bonus room that can be used to the homeowners discretion.

REAR ELEVATION

KITCHEN: The serving bar in this spacious kitchen is the perfect place for homework or impromptu meals.

MASTER SUITE: Modified from the original, a sitting room was added to this master suite.

HOME OFFICE/BEDROOM 4: The perfect flexible space, these homeowners chose to use this as a music conservatory.

MASTER BATH: The granite countertops and contemporary sinks showcase the homeowners taste.

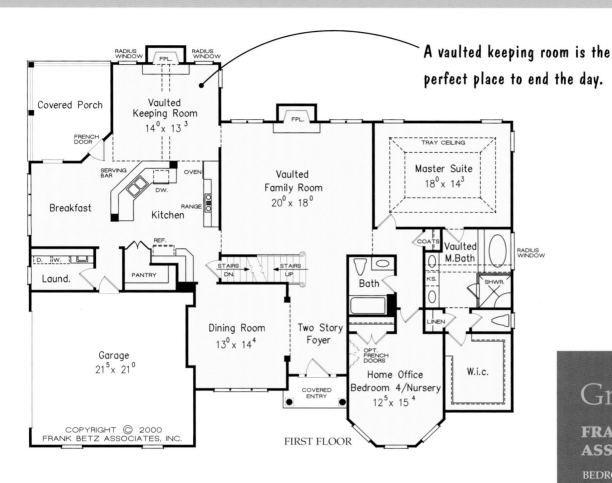

A vaulted keeping room is the perfect place to end the day.

Covered Porch

RADIUS WINDOW · FPL. · RADIUS WINDOW

Vaulted Keeping Room
14^0 x 13^3

FRENCH DOOR

SERVING BAR

Breakfast

Kitchen · DW. · OVEN · RANGE

Vaulted Family Room
20^0 x 18^0

FPL.

TRAY CEILING

Master Suite
18^0 x 14^3

RADIUS WINDOW

COATS

Vaulted M.Bath

KS.

SHWR.

LINEN

Bath

REF.

D. · W.

Laund.

PANTRY

STAIRS DN. · STAIRS UP

Dining Room
13^0 x 14^4

Garage
21^5 x 21^0

Two Story Foyer

OPT. FRENCH DOORS

Home Office Bedroom 4/Nursery
12^5 x 15^4

W.i.c.

COVERED ENTRY

COPYRIGHT © 2000
FRANK BETZ ASSOCIATES, INC.

FIRST FLOOR

PRICING FOR SDHFB01-3559

Sets	Price
1	$945
5	$995
8	$1045
VELLUM	$1295
CD	$2245

Greenlaw

FRANK BETZ ASSOCIATES, INC.

BEDROOMS 4
BATH 4
WIDTH . . . . 64'0"
DEPTH. . . . . 55'2"
1ST FLOOR. . . . . 2247 sq ft
2ND FLOOR. . . . . 637 sq ft
LIVING AREA . . . . 2884 sq ft
OPT. BONUS ROOM. . . 235 sq ft
FOUNDATION. . . . . CRAWL SPACE, SLAB OR BASEMENT
PLAN NUMBER **SDHFB01-3559**

Family Room Below

VAULT

Loft
OVERLOOK

W.i.c.

Bedroom 3
12^4 x 12^0

LINEN

OPEN RAIL

STAIRS DN.

POCKET DOOR

Bath

Bath

Bedroom 2
12^0 x 12^0

Foyer Below

Opt. Bonus
12^0 x 15^{10}

This bonus room allows the homeowner to finish this space as they wish.

SECOND FLOOR

KITCHEN: The inviting kitchen—complete with a double oven, pantry and rows of Shaker-style cherry cabinets—will make even a novice cook feel like a chef.

GREAT ROOM: Creating its own work of art, ornamental paned windows and glass doors open onto a covered porch, where breathtaking views are uninterrupted. A cozy fireplace warms the spacious room.

DINING AREA: Artfully decorated, the common living spaces blend together seamlessly. A square archway frames the sitting area beyond the dining room.

Santa Rosa

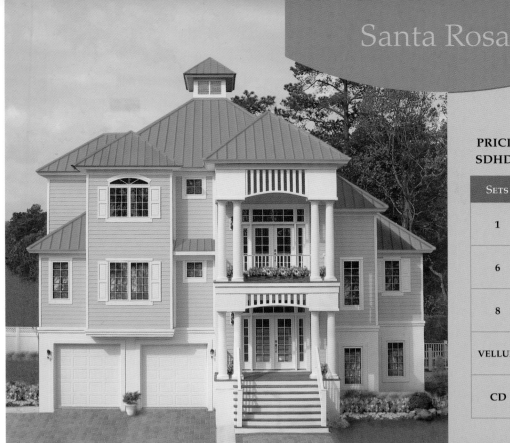

PRICING FOR
SDHDS01-6808

Sets	Price
1	N/A
6	$1187
8	N/A
VELLUM	$1187
CD	$2176

THE SATER DESIGN COLLECTION, INC.

BEDROOMS 3
BATH 2
WIDTH . . . . 48'0"
DEPTH. . . . . 42'0"
1ST FLOOR. . . . . 1383 sq ft
2ND FLOOR. . . . . 595 sq ft
LIVING AREA . . . . 1978 sq ft
FOUNDATION. . . . . . . ISLAND BASEMENT
PLAN NUMBER. **SDHDS01-6808**

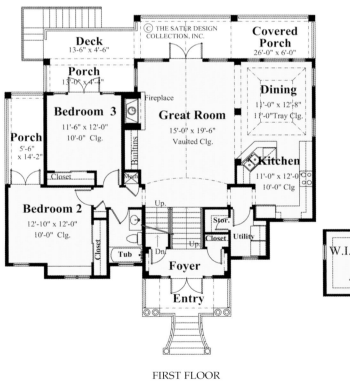

FIRST FLOOR

SECOND FLOOR

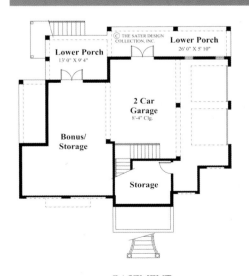

BASEMENT

© 2001 Frank Betz Associates, Inc

PRICING FOR SDHFB01-3612

Sets	Price
1	$810
5	$860
8	$910
Vellum	$1095
CD	$1895

Rear Elevation

Please, come in...No one can turn that invitation down once they see this design. Living and dining rooms grace each side of the foyer. A coffered ceiling canopies the grand room, with a fireplace and transom window as its backdrop. Sunshine beams into the breakfast area through a wall of windows, making this the perfect spot to start the day.

Bosworth

FRANK BETZ ASSOCIATES, INC.

BEDROOMS 4
BATH 3-1/2
WIDTH . . . . 61'0"
DEPTH . . . . 58'6"
1ST FLOOR . . . . 2296 sq ft
LIVING AREA . . . . 2296 sq ft
OPT. 2ND FLOOR . . . . . 286 sq ft
FOUNDATION . . . . CRAWL SPACE, SLAB
OR BASEMENT
PLAN NUMBER **SDHFB01-3612**

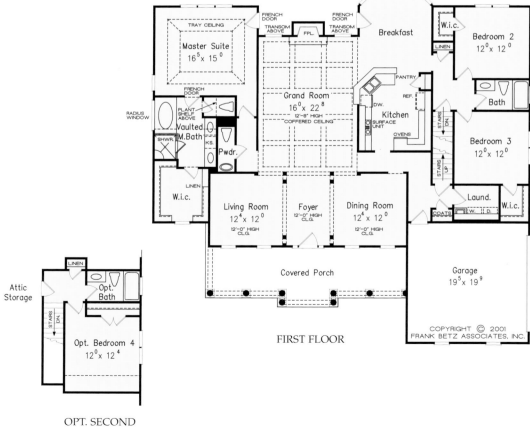

OPT. SECOND
FLOOR

FIRST FLOOR

COPYRIGHT © 2001
FRANK BETZ ASSOCIATES, INC.

© 2003 Donald A. Gardner, Inc.

PRICING FOR SDHDG01-1022

Sets	Price
1	$620
5	$680
8	$730
VELLUM	$1025
CD	$1850

REAR ELEVATION

FIRST FLOOR

PORCH

BED RM.
11-4 x 11-4

fireplace

GREAT RM.
16-8 x 16-8
(cathedral ceiling)

shelves

BRKFST.
11-8 x 10-4
(cathedral ceiling)

MASTER BED RM.
15-0 x 13-10

walk-in closet

up

master bath

seat

UTIL.

w   d

bath

cl

KIT.
9-0 x 13-0

BED RM.
11-4 x 11-4

cl

FOYER
5-0 x 11-4

cl

DINING
13-8 x 11-4

GARAGE
22-0 x 22-0

© 2003 DONALD A. GARDNER
All rights reserved

STORAGE

PORCH

BONUS RM.
14-0 x 22-0

attic storage

down

attic storage

attic storage

A welcoming front porch with bold columns and gables with decorative brackets add tremendous curb appeal to this home. A sidelight and elliptical transom usher natural light into the foyer, and the open floor plan creates family-efficiency. A single column and elegant tray ceiling distinguishes the dining room without enclosing space, while a built-in cabinet is positioned next to the fireplace.

Violet

DONALD A. GARDNER ARCHITECTS, INC.

BEDROOMS 3
BATH 2
WIDTH . . . . 65'4"
DEPTH . . . . 48'8"
1ST FLOOR . . . . 1660 sq ft
LIVING AREA . . . . 1660 sq ft
BONUS ROOM . . . . 374 sq ft
FOUNDATION . . . . CRAWL SPACE*
PLAN NUMBER SDHDG01-1016

*Other options available. See page 175.

PRICING FOR SDHFB01-3915

Sets	Price
1	$685
5	$735
8	$785
VELLUM	$905
CD	$1555

REAR ELEVATION

The façade of the *River Hill* is like a friendly invitation to come in and see more. A vaulted family room is the focal point from the foyer, with a cozy fireplace as its backdrop. Finishing the optional second floor adds a bedroom and bath, as well as a bonus room that can be used to the homeowner's discretion.

River Hill

FRANK BETZ ASSOCIATES, INC.

BEDROOMS	4
BATH	3
WIDTH	54'0"
DEPTH	54'0"
1ST FLOOR	1656 sq ft
LIVING AREA	1656 sq ft
OPT. 2ND FLOOR	717 sq ft
FOUNDATION	CRAWL SPACE, SLAB OR BASEMENT
PLAN NUMBER	**SDHFB01-3915**

PRICING FOR
SDHDS01-8071

SETS	PRICE
1	N/A
6	$1315
8	N/A
VELLUM	$1315
CD	$2410

REAR ELEVATION

The Sater Design Collection, Inc.

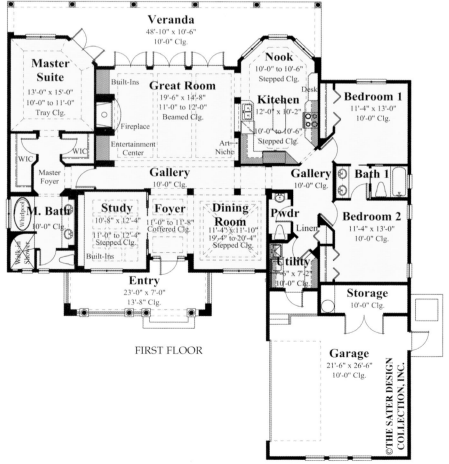

Veranda
48'-10" x 10'-6"
10'-0" Clg.

Master Suite
13'-0" x 15'-0"
10'-0" to 11'-0"
Tray Clg.

Built-Ins

Great Room
19'-6" x 14'-8"
11'-0" to 12'-0"
Beamed Clg.

Nook
10'-0" to 10'-6"
Stepped Clg.

Desk

Kitchen
12'-0" x 10'-2"
10'-0" to 10'-6"
Stepped Clg.

Bedroom 1
11'-4" x 13'-0"
10'-0" Clg.

Fireplace

Entertainment Center

WIC

WIC

Art-Niche

Gallery
10'-0" Clg.

Gallery
10'-0" Clg.

Bath 1

Master Foyer

M. Bath
10'-0" Clg.

Whirlpool

Study
10'-8" x 12'-4"
11'-0" to 12'-4"
Stepped Clg.

Built-Ins

Walk-in Shower

Foyer
11'-0" to 11'-8"
Coffered Clg.

Dining Room
11'-4" x 11'-10"
19'-4" to 20'-4"
Stepped Clg.

Pwdr

Linen

Bedroom 2
11'-4" x 13'-0"
10'-0" Clg.

Utility
x 7'-2"
10'-0" Clg.

Entry
23'-0" x 7'-0"
13'-8" Clg.

Storage
10'-0" Clg.

FIRST FLOOR

Garage
21'-6" x 26'-6"
10'-0" Clg.

©THE SATER DESIGN COLLECTION, INC.

Columns, stucco and rough-hewn stone embellish the façade of this charming Tuscan villa. Inside, a beamed ceiling contributes a sense of spaciousness to the heart of the home, while walls of glass draw the outdoors in. Varied ceiling treatments and arches define the open interior, permitting flexibility as well as great views. The great room is anchored by a fireplace flanked by built-in shelves and an entertainment center, visible from the kitchen via a pass-thru.

Casina Rossa

THE SATER DESIGN COLLECTION, INC.

BEDROOMS 3
BATH 2-1/2
WIDTH . . . . 62'10"
DEPTH . . . . 73'6"
1ST FLOOR . . . . 2191 sq ft
LIVING AREA . . . . 2191 sq ft
FOUNDATION . . . . SLAB
PLAN NUMBER **SDHDS01-8071**

PRICING FOR SDHVA01-9031

SETS	PRICE
VELLUM	$2095
PRINTABLE PDF ON DISK	$1795

The best of the past and present combine in this perfectly planned Arts-and-Crafts-inspired family home. Attention to detail is seen throughout -- from the exterior siding to the interior built-ins and details. The first floor includes a large living room with a fireplace and a spacious kitchen, while the second floor includes three large bedrooms, including a master bedroom suite. An additional guest bedroom and a family room complete the lower level.

Spencer

VISBEEN ASSOCIATES, INC.

BEDROOMS 4
BATH 3-1/2
WIDTH . . . . 65'0"
DEPTH . . . . 32'0"
1ST FLOOR . . . . 993 sq ft
2ND FLOOR . . . . 936 sq ft
LIVING AREA . . . . 1929 sq ft
OPT. BASEMENT . . . . . 701 sq ft
FOUNDATION . . . . VIEWOUT
PLAN NUMBER **SDHVA01-9031**

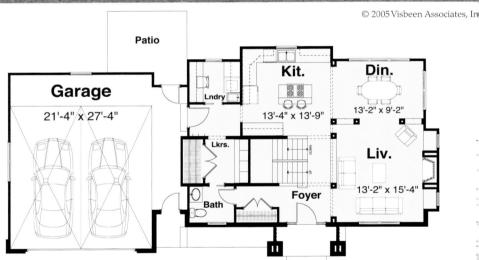

FIRST FLOOR

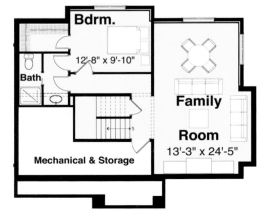

OPT. BASEMENT

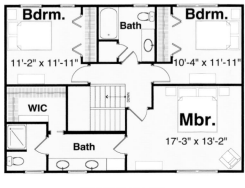

SECOND FLOOR

PRICING FOR SDHDG01-1015

SETS	PRICE
1	$620
5	$680
8	$730
VELLUM	$1025
CD	$1850

REAR ELEVATION

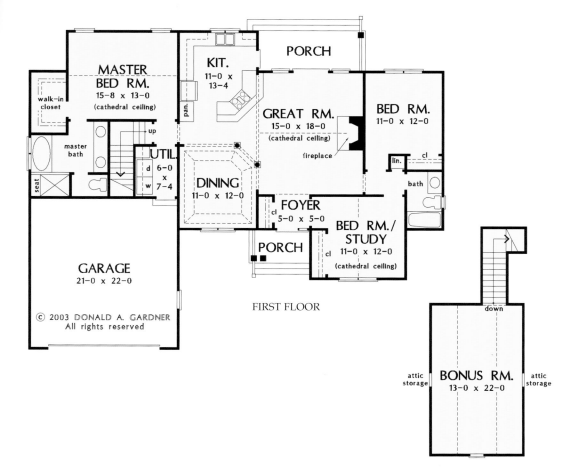

MASTER BED RM.
15-8 x 13-0
(cathedral ceiling)

walk-in closet

master bath

seat

UTIL
d 6-0
w 7-4
x

up

KIT.
11-0 x 13-4

pan.

PORCH

GREAT RM.
15-0 x 18-0
(cathedral ceiling)

fireplace

BED RM.
11-0 x 12-0

lin. cl

bath

DINING
11-0 x 12-0

FOYER
cl 5-0 x 5-0

GARAGE
21-0 x 22-0

BED RM./ STUDY
11-0 x 12-0
(cathedral ceiling)

cl

PORCH

FIRST FLOOR

down

attic storage

BONUS RM.
13-0 x 22-0

attic storage

This family-efficient floor plan is designed as a step-saver and allows a natural traffic flow. While a bonus room and study/bedroom provide flexibility, custom-styled features include a cathedral ceiling in the master bedroom, study/bedroom and great room, along with a tray ceiling in the dining room. An angled cooktop counter and columns keep the common rooms open. The fireplace adds ambiance.

Hilligan

DONALD A. GARDNER ARCHITECTS, INC.

BEDROOMS 3
BATH 2
WIDTH . . . . 59'8"
DEPTH. . . . . 47'4"
1ST FLOOR. . . . . 1535 sq ft
LIVING AREA . . . . 1535 sq ft
BONUS ROOM. . . . . . . 355 sq ft
FOUNDATION. . . . . . . CRAWL SPACE*
PLAN NUMBER. **SDHDG01-1015**

*Other options available. See page 175.

PRICING FOR SDHDS01-6771

SETS	PRICE
1	N/A
6	$1270
8	N/A
VELLUM	$1270
CD	$2329

REAR ELEVATION

© The Sater Design Collection, In

The large leisure room, with its wall of built-ins and open connection to a corner eating nook and gourmet kitchen, make this home ideal for families of every size. An elegant dining room sits just off the foyer and across from the formal living room. Retreating glass walls expand both the nook and living room to the verandah, making indoor/outdoor entertaining effortless.

Aldwin

THE SATER DESIGN COLLECTION, INC.

BEDROOMS 3
BATH 2
WIDTH . . . . 60'8"
DEPTH. . . . . 59'10"
1ST FLOOR. . . . . 2117 sq ft
LIVING AREA . . . . 2117 sq ft
FOUNDATION. . . . . . . SLAB
PLAN NUMBER **SDHDS01-6771**

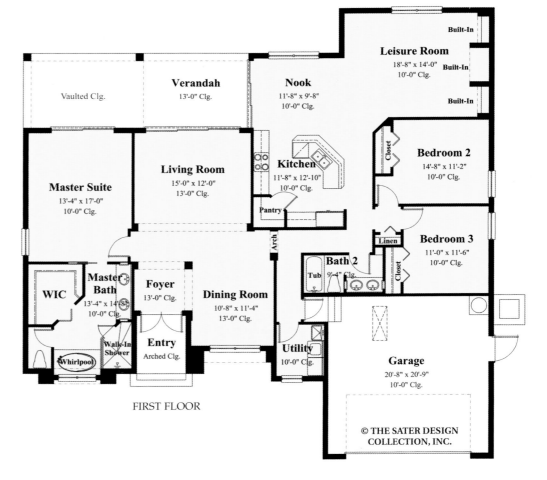

FIRST FLOOR

© THE SATER DESIGN COLLECTION, INC.

© 2002 Frank Betz Associates, Inc.

PRICING FOR
SDHFB01-3668

SETS	PRICE
1	$745
5	$795
8	$845
VELLUM	$995
CD	$1720

REAR ELEVATION

FIRST FLOOR

FRENCH DOOR
FPL
VAULT
Vaulted Breakfast
SERVING BAR
TRAY CEILING
Master Suite 16⁵ x 13⁰
PANT.
Vaulted Family Room 16⁶ x 16⁸
RANGE
DW
KITCHEN
REF.
PASS THRU
STAIRS UP
K.S.
M.Bath
STAIRS DN.
COATS
SHWR
LINEN
Two Story Foyer
W.i.c.
Vaulted Dining Room 11⁰ x 11⁶
Pwdr.
W D
Laund.
Covered Porch
Garage 20⁵ x 19⁹

COPYRIGHT © 2002 FRANK BETZ ASSOCIATES, INC.

SECOND FLOOR

Family Room Below
VAULT
Bedroom 3 12⁰ x 12⁰
W.i.c.
W.i.c.
OPEN RAIL
Bedroom 2 11⁶ x 11⁴
OPEN RAIL
STAIRS DN.
LINEN
Bath
Opt. W.i.c.
PLANT SHELF
Opt. Bonus 12⁵ x 19⁹

Volume makes this home feel larger than it is, with vaulted, tray and two-story ceilings throughout the main level. Day-to-day living is easier because of the attention to details in the design process. A linen closet is situated within the master bedroom closet. The laundry area can also be a mudroom with its direct access off the garage. A handy pass-through from the kitchen to the great room makes entertaining easier.

Rivermeade

FRANK BETZ ASSOCIATES, INC.

BEDROOMS 3
BATH 2-1/2
WIDTH . . . . 45'0"
DEPTH . . . . 52'4"
1ST FLOOR . . . . 1359 sq ft
2ND FLOOR . . . . 520 sq ft
LIVING AREA . . . . 1879 sq ft
OPT. BONUS ROOM . . . 320 sq ft
FOUNDATION . . . . CRAWL SPACE OR BASEMENT
PLAN NUMBER **SDHFB01-3668**

PRICING FOR SDHDG01-968

SETS	PRICE
1	$575
5	$630
8	$685
VELLUM	$960
CD	$1720

REAR ELEVATION

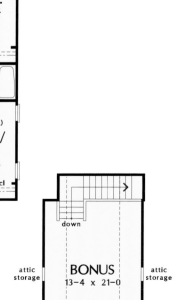

Poised and cozy, this home features a split bedroom plan. The floor plan is family-efficient and has a variety of custom-styled touches, such as tray ceilings in the dining room and master bedroom. The great room is highlighted by a cathedral ceiling, fireplace and French doors that lead to the rear porch. The convenient front-entry garage has a bonus room above it.

Oakway

DONALD A. GARDNER ARCHITECTS, INC.

BEDROOMS 3
BATH 2
WIDTH . . . . 50'4"
DEPTH . . . . 46'4"
1ST FLOOR . . . . 1457 sq ft
LIVING AREA . . . . 1457 sq ft
BONUS ROOM . . . . 341 sq ft
FOUNDATION . . . . CRAWL SPACE*
PLAN NUMBER **SDHDG01-968**

*Other options available. See page 175.

FIRST FLOOR

- walk-in closet
- MASTER BED RM. 12-0 x 14-0
- BRKFST. 9-0 x 8-0
- PORCH
- GREAT RM. 13-4 x 16-4
- BED RM. 11-4 x 12-4
- UTIL. 5-8 x 6-4 d w
- KIT. 8-4 x 9-0
- master bath
- fireplace
- (cathedral ceiling)
- cl
- bath
- up
- DINING 11-4 x 12-0
- FOYER 5-0 x 11-0
- (vaulted ceiling)
- BED RM./ STUDY 11-4 x 11-8
- GARAGE 21-0 x 21-0
- PORCH
- cl
- seat
- cl

BONUS 13-4 x 21-0

- down
- attic storage
- attic storage

© The Sater Design Collection, Inc.

REAR ELEVATION

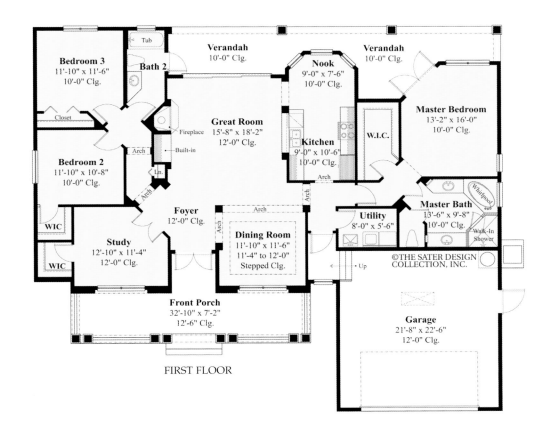

Bedroom 3
11'-10" x 11'-6"
10'-0" Clg.

Tub

Bath 2

Verandah
10'-0" Clg.

Nook
9'-0" x 7'-6"
10'-0" Clg.

Verandah
10'-0" Clg.

Closet

Great Room
15'-8" x 18'-2"
12'-0" Clg.

Fireplace

Built-in

Kitchen
9'-0" x 10'-6"
10'-0" Clg.

W.I.C.

Master Bedroom
13'-2" x 16'-0"
10'-0" Clg.

Bedroom 2
11'-10" x 10'-8"
10'-0" Clg.

Arch

Ln.

Arch

Foyer
12'-0" Clg.

Arch

WIC

Study
12'-10" x 11'-4"
12'-0" Clg.

WIC

Arch

Dining Room
11'-10" x 11'-6"
11'-4" to 12'-0"
Stepped Clg.

Arch

Arch

Utility
8'-0" x 5'-6"

Whirlpool

Master Bath
13'-6" x 9'-8"
10'-0" Clg.

Walk-In
Shower

©THE SATER DESIGN
COLLECTION, INC.

Front Porch
32'-10" x 7'-2"
12'-6" Clg.

• Up

Garage
21'-8" x 22'-6"
12'-0" Clg.

FIRST FLOOR

Find classic charm in the multi-pane windows, double columns and multiple dormers of this country home. *Maywood* is an especially open floor plan with large dining, kitchen and great rooms divided by columns and arches. Extending the living space outside, retreating glass walls open the great room to the veranda. This split bedroom plan affords easy privacy for the master suite and two secondary bedrooms.

Maywood

THE SATER DESIGN COLLECTION, INC.

BEDROOMS 3
BATH 2
WIDTH . . . . 64'0"
DEPTH . . . . 55'0"
1ST FLOOR . . . . 1911 sq ft
LIVING AREA . . . . 1911 sq ft
FOUNDATION . . . . CRAWL SPACE
PLAN NUMBER **SDHDS01-6776**

PRICING FOR SDHDS01-7005

SETS	PRICE
1	N/A
6	$1492
8	N/A
VELLUM	$1492
CD	$2736

REAR ELEVATION

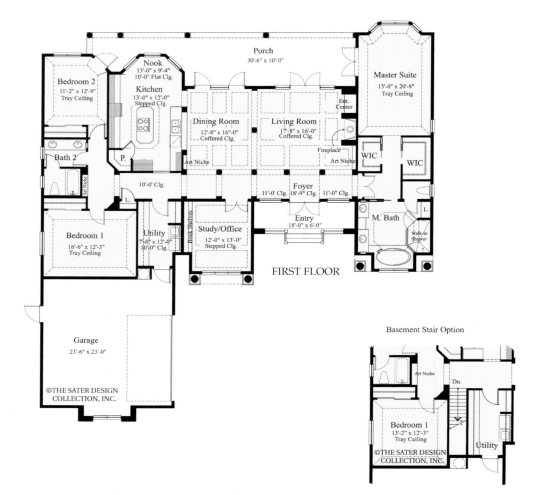

© The Sater Design Collection, Inc

An expansive rear porch and a recessed arch-covered entryway are the highlights of the *Marcella*. Inside, more columns and coffered ceilings provide understated elegance to the living and dining rooms. With its handy pass-thru to the dining room, the kitchen also features a walk-in pantry and spacious nook. Both the office and master suite boast refreshing views through the wide windows.

Marcella

THE SATER DESIGN COLLECTION, INC.

BEDROOMS	3
BATH	2
WIDTH	70'0"
DEPTH	72'0"
1ST FLOOR	2487 sq ft
LIVING AREA	2487 sq ft
FOUNDATION	SLAB OR OPT. BASEMENT
PLAN NUMBER	SDHDS01-7005

© 2000 Donald A. Gardner, Inc.

PRICING FOR SDHDG01-889

SETS	PRICE
1	$575
5	$630
8	$685
VELLUM	$960
CD	$1720

REAR ELEVATION

Cathedral ceilings top the great room, dining room, master bedroom and a secondary bedroom. Without taking away space, the angled island separates the kitchen from the dining room and great room. Built-ins and a stunning fireplace highlight the great room, which accesses the deck. With a garden tub framed by two windows, the master bath has its share of light.

Larchmont

DONALD A. GARDNER ARCHITECTS, INC.

BEDROOMS 3
BATH 2
WIDTH . . . . 66'4"
DEPTH . . . . 36'6"
1ST FLOOR . . . . 1309 sq ft
LIVING AREA . . . . 1309 sq ft
FOUNDATION . . . . CRAWL SPACE*
PLAN NUMBER SDHDG01-889

DECK

walk-in closet

MASTER BED RM.
11-4 x 15-0
(cathedral ceiling)

master bath

bath

cl

BED RM.
10-0 x 10-0

BED RM.
10-0 x 10-0
(cathedral ceiling)

cl

GREAT RM.
14-0 x 15-0

DINING
10-0 x 10-0
(cathedral ceiling)

fireplace
shelves

w   d

cl

FOYER
6-8 x 7-8

KIT.
9-8 x 13-8

GARAGE
20-8 x 21-4

PORCH

© 2000 DONALD A. GARDNER
All rights reserved

FIRST FLOOR

*Other options available. See page 175.

PRICING FOR
SDHGA01-00186

Sets	Price
1	N/A
5	$1095
8	N/A
VELLUM	$1195
CD	$2045

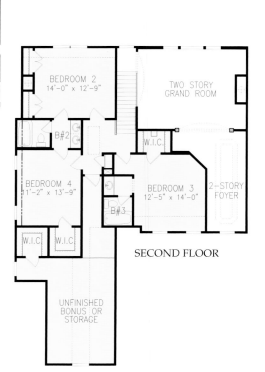

© 2000-2007 Garrell Associates, Inc

REAR ELEVATION

Comfortable living for a family of any size, the *Turnberry* is a courtyard design with a lovely front porch. Featured is a master suite on the main floor and a keeping, breakfast and kitchen area suitable for large gatherings. The second floor is complete with three bedrooms and a spacious bonus room.

Turnberry

GARRELL ASSOCIATES, INC.

BEDROOMS 4
BATH 3-1/2
WIDTH . . . . 54'0"
DEPTH . . . . 64'0"
1ST FLOOR . . . . 1878 sq ft
2ND FLOOR . . . . 826 sq ft
LIVING AREA . . . . 2704 sq ft
BONUS ROOM . . . . 357 sq ft
FOUNDATION . . . . BASEMENT OR SLAB
PLAN NUMBER **SDHGA01-00186**

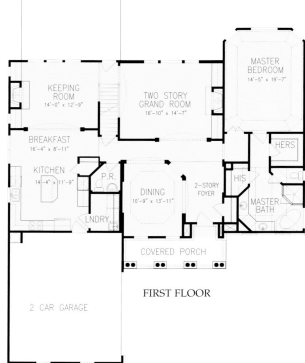

FIRST FLOOR

SECOND FLOOR

© 1997 Frank Betz Associates, Inc.

REAR ELEVATION

FIRST FLOOR

TRAY CEILING

Master Suite
13⁶ x 15⁰

FPL.

VAULT

Breakfast

OPT. BAY

FRENCH DOOR

W.i.c.

LINEN

Bedroom 3
11¹ x 11⁰

Vaulted Great Room
14⁰ x 19⁰
14'-0" CLG. HT.

SERVING BAR

REF.

Bath

Kitchen

DW.

RANGE

PANTRY

Bedroom 2
11³ x 11¹

RADIUS WINDOW

FRENCH DOOR

Vaulted M.Bath

STAIRS UP

W. D.

Laund.

Foyer
14'-0" CLG. HT.

ARCHED OPENING

Dining Room
11⁰ x 11⁰

SHWR.

PLANT SHELF ABOVE

LINEN

W.i.c.

COATS

VAULT

DECORATIVE COLUMNS

OPT. STAIRS TO BSMT.

Covered Porch

Garage
20⁵ x 22³

COPYRIGHT © 1997
FRANK BETZ ASSOCIATES, INC.

GARAGE LOCATION WITH BASEMENT

OPT. SECOND FLOOR

STAIRS DN.

Opt. Bonus
12⁵ x 22³

The *Jasmine* has that friendly, cottage-like appeal with its calm combination of natural stone and siding. A simple, uncomplicated design is what you'll find inside. The kitchen and breakfast room adjoin the great room, graced with a vaulted ceiling. The master suite encompasses the left wing of the home. Careful placement of the guest bath between the secondary bedrooms creates a comfortable separation from each other for added privacy.

Jasmine

FRANK BETZ ASSOCIATES, INC.

BEDROOMS 3
BATH 2
WIDTH . . . . 53'6"
DEPTH . . . . 55'10"
1ST FLOOR . . . . 1604 sq ft
LIVING AREA . . . . 1604 sq ft
OPT. 2ND FLOOR . . . . . 288 sq ft
FOUNDATION . . . . CRAWL SPACE, SLAB OR BASEMENT
PLAN NUMBER SDHFB01-1036

© 2005 Frank Betz Associates, Inc

PRICING FOR
SDHFB01-3919

SETS	PRICE
1	$745
5	$795
8	$845
VELLUM	$995
CD	$1720

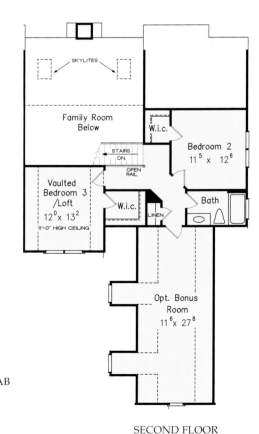

REAR ELEVATION

Especially designed for small and corner lots the *Stoneleigh Cottage* offers amenities usually reserved for much larger homes. Inside, the open floor plan allows for easy flow between rooms, making entertaining a breeze. The master suite encompasses one wing of the home. This suite has a back wall of windows allowing in both natural light and rear views

Stoneleigh Cottage

FRANK BETZ ASSOCIATES, INC.

BEDROOMS	3
BATH	2-1/2
WIDTH	46'0"
DEPTH	62'4"
1ST FLOOR	1448 sq ft
2ND FLOOR	527 sq ft
LIVING AREA	1975 sq ft
OPT. BONUS ROOM	368 sq ft
FOUNDATION	CRAWL SPACE, SLAB OR BASEMENT
PLAN NUMBER	**SDHFB01-3919**

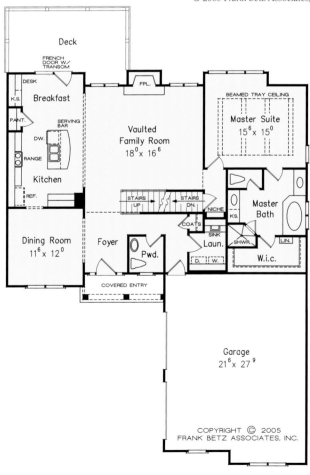

SECOND FLOOR

FIRST FLOOR

COPYRIGHT © 2005
FRANK BETZ ASSOCIATES, INC.

PRICING FOR
SDHDS01-6644

SETS	PRICE
1	N/A
6	$1432
8	N/A
VELLUM	$1432
CD	$2626

© The Sater Design Collection, Inc.

REAR ELEVATION

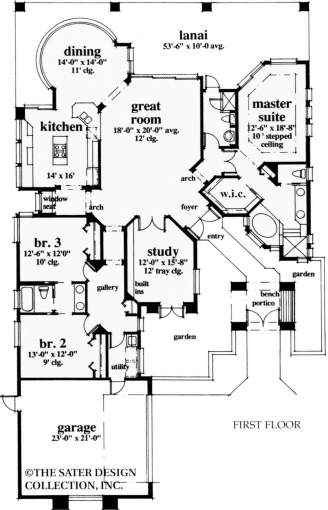

A gated portico leads into the courtyard and entrance of this charming home. Inside, the foyer opens to the great room, which further expands through retreating glass walls to the lanai. An arched entryway leads to the formal dining room and well-appointed kitchen. Down the gallery hall are two guest suites. On the opposite side of the home, the master retreat enjoys privacy and many luxe amenities.

Dorado

THE SATER DESIGN COLLECTION, INC.

BEDROOMS 3
BATH 3
WIDTH . . . . 53'6"
DEPTH . . . . 94'6"
1ST FLOOR . . . . 2387 sq ft
LIVING AREA . . . . 2387 sq ft
FOUNDATION . . . . SLAB
PLAN NUMBER **SDHDS01-6644**

FIRST FLOOR

©THE SATER DESIGN COLLECTION, INC.

PRICING FOR SDHFB01-3694

SETS	PRICE
1	$685
5	$735
8	$785
VELLUM	$905
CD	$1555

© 2002 Frank Betz Associates, Inc.

REAR ELEVATION

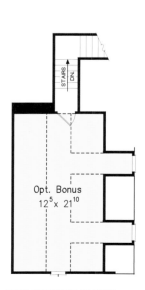

Copper window accents, brick and an arched-covered entry come together to create a warm *Brookhollow* welcome. The main living area is airy and unobtrusive, with columns serving as the border of the dining room. Radius windows on each side of the fireplace allow the natural light to pour into this living space.

Brookhollow

FRANK BETZ ASSOCIATES, INC.

BEDROOMS 3
BATH 2
WIDTH . . . . 54'0"
DEPTH. . . . . 59'6"
1ST FLOOR. . . . . 1768 sq ft
LIVING AREA . . . . 1768 sq ft
OPT. 2ND FLOOR. . . . . 354 sq ft
FOUNDATION. . . . . . . CRAWL SPACE, SLAB OR BASEMENT
PLAN NUMBER. **SDHFB01-3694**

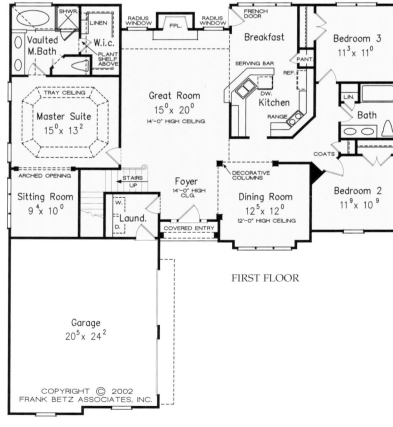

FIRST FLOOR

COPYRIGHT © 2002
FRANK BETZ ASSOCIATES, INC.

OPT. SECOND FLOOR

PRICING FOR SDHDG01-946

SETS	PRICE
1	$575
5	$630
8	$685
VELLUM	$960
CD	$1720

REAR ELEVATION

2001 Donald A. Gardner, Inc.

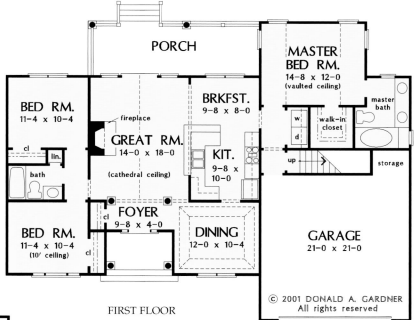

PORCH

BED RM.
11-4 x 10-4

cl | lin.

fireplace

GREAT RM.
14-0 x 18-0
(cathedral ceiling)

BRKFST.
9-8 x 8-0

KIT.
9-8 x 10-0

MASTER BED RM.
14-8 x 12-0
(vaulted ceiling)

master bath

w
d

walk-in closet

up

storage

bath

BED RM.
11-4 x 10-4
(10' ceiling)

cl

FOYER
9-8 x 4-0

cl

DINING
12-0 x 10-4

GARAGE
21-0 x 21-0

FIRST FLOOR

attic storage

down

BONUS RM.
13-4 x 21-0

attic storage

Above the front door, a fanlight emphasizes the arch of the Palladian-styled window, along with the window in the bonus room and gable. While columns are used to define the foyer, a tray ceiling crowns the dining room. The great room boasts a cathedral ceiling, striking fireplace and French doors that lead outside. The master suite is designed to pamper.

Keegan

DONALD A. GARDNER ARCHITECTS, INC.

BEDROOMS 3
BATH 2
WIDTH . . . . 57'8"
DEPTH . . . . 44'0"
1ST FLOOR . . . . 1377 sq ft
LIVING AREA . . . . 1377 sq ft
BONUS ROOM . . . . 322 sq ft
FOUNDATION . . . . CRAWL SPACE*
PLAN NUMBER **SDHDG01-946**

*Other options available. See page 175.

PRICING FOR SDHFB01-3662

Sets	Price
1	$745
5	$795
8	$845
VELLUM	$995
CD	$1720

© 2002 Frank Betz Associates, In

REAR ELEVATION

Stone accents, carriage doors and board-and-batten shutters come together to create the cottage-like appeal that is so desirable today. An art niche is positioned as a focal point in the foyer, where continuous arched openings separate and define the dining area. The master suite is private and secluded, encompassing an entire wing of the main level.

Stonechase

FRANK BETZ ASSOCIATES, INC.

BEDROOMS	3
BATH	2-1/2
WIDTH	50'0"
DEPTH	46'0"
1ST FLOOR	1458 sq ft
2ND FLOOR	516 sq ft
LIVING AREA	1974 sq ft
OPT. BONUS ROOM	168 sq ft
FOUNDATION	CRAWL SPACE OR BASEMENT
PLAN NUMBER	**SDHFB01-3662**

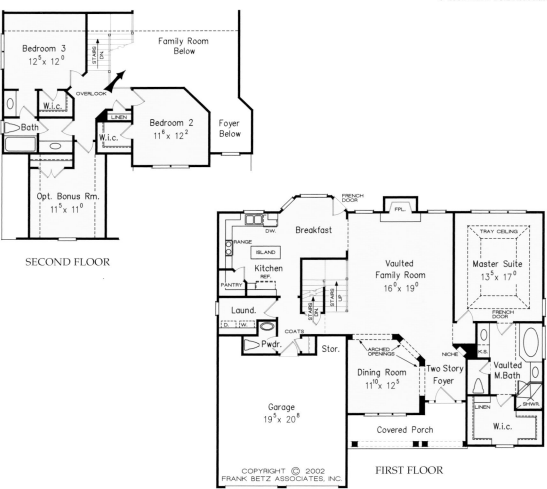

SECOND FLOOR

FIRST FLOOR

COPYRIGHT © 2002
FRANK BETZ ASSOCIATES, INC.

PRICING FOR
SDHDS01-7050

SETS	PRICE
1	N/A
6	$1533
8	N/A
VELLUM	$1533
CD	$2810

REAR ELEVATION

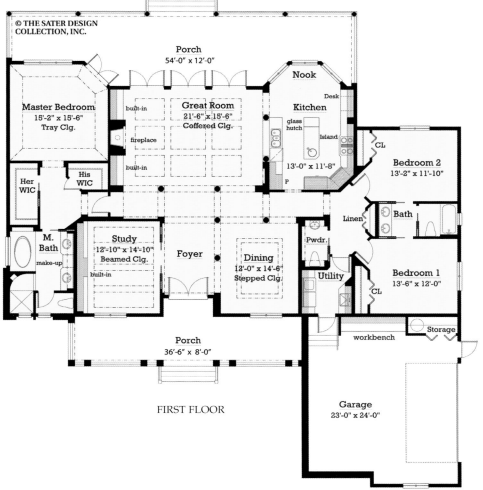

FIRST FLOOR

An impressive gable supplies the focal point for a charming façade with handsome slumped arches. *Lunden Valley* is an especially open floor plan with large dining, kitchen and great rooms divided by columns. Three sets of French doors open the great room to the back porch; another set is found in the master bedroom. This split-floor plan affords easy privacy for the master suite and two guest bedrooms.

Lunden Valley

THE SATER DESIGN COLLECTION, INC.

BEDROOMS 3
BATH 2-1/2
WIDTH . . . . 70'6"
DEPTH . . . . 76'6"
1ST FLOOR . . . . 2555 sq ft
LIVING AREA . . . . 2555 sq ft
FOUNDATION . . . . CRAWL SPACE
PLAN NUMBER **SDHDS01-7050**

PRICING FOR
SDHDG01-384

Sets	Price
1	$620
5	$680
8	$730
VELLUM	$1025
CD	$1850

REAR ELEVATION

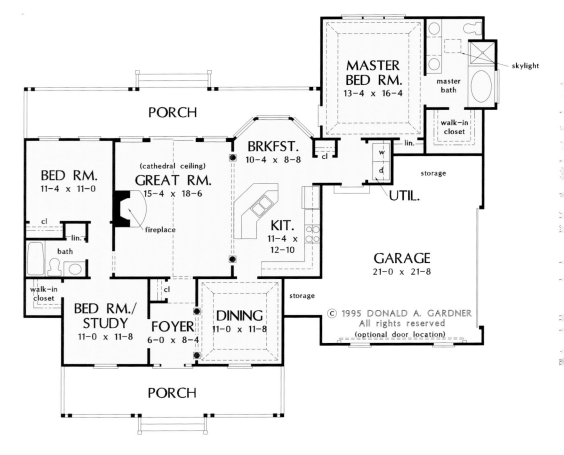

From its wide front porch to its front swing room, this home has all the extras that today's families are looking for. The floor plan maximizes square footage with its openness and efficient use of space. The great room features clerestory windows, a cathedral ceiling and French doors that access a porch. The private master suite is designed to pamper.

Stratford

DONALD A. GARDNER ARCHITECTS, INC.

BEDROOMS 3
BATH 2
WIDTH . . . . 62'4"
DEPTH . . . . 55'2"
1ST FLOOR . . . . 1632 sq ft
LIVING AREA . . . . 1632 sq ft
FOUNDATION . . . . CRAWL SPACE*
PLAN NUMBER **SDHDG01-384**

PORCH

MASTER BED RM.
13-4 x 16-4

skylight

master bath

walk-in closet

BRKFST.
10-4 x 8-8

cl

storage

(cathedral ceiling)

GREAT RM.
15-4 x 18-6

BED RM.
11-4 x 11-0

lin.

w
d

UTIL.

cl

fireplace

KIT.
11-4 x 12-10

bath

GARAGE
21-0 x 21-8

walk-in closet

(optional door location)

BED RM./
STUDY
11-0 x 11-8

FOYER
6-0 x 8-4

cl

DINING
11-0 x 11-8

storage

PORCH

FIRST FLOOR

*Other options available. See page 175.

© 2002 Frank Betz Associates, Inc.

PRICING FOR
SDHFB01-3666

Sets	Price
1	$745
5	$795
8	$845
VELLUM	$995
CD	$1720

REAR ELEVATION

OPT. SITTING ROOM

Sitting Area 10⁰ x 10⁰

Master Suite 16⁷ x 13⁵

FIRST FLOOR

FRENCH DOORS

SERVING BAR

RANGE   DW.

Kitchen

REF.

Breakfast

FPL.

Family Room 19⁰ x 13⁵

DECORATIVE COLUMN OVER KNEEWALL

LIN

PANT.

Laund.

Pwdr.

COATS

D.   W.

STAIRS DN.

Dining Room 11⁷ x 12⁰

STAIRS UP

Two Story Foyer

Garage 19⁵ x 22⁹

Covered Porch

COPYRIGHT © 2002
FRANK BETZ ASSOCIATES, INC.

SECOND FLOOR

Bedroom 3 11⁰ x 11⁶

Bedroom 4 10⁰ x 10⁰

TRAY CEILING

Master Suite 16⁷ x 13⁵

Bath

LINEN

OPEN RAIL

STAIRS DN.

SHWR.

W.i.c.

Vaulted M.Bath

LINEN

RADIUS WINDOW

Bedroom 2 11⁷ x 11⁰

Foyer Below

K.S.

PLANT SHELF

Simply elegant outside and in, the *Bentridge* is well planned and functional. Four bedrooms share the upper level. Ornamental columns and knee walls offset the family room, separating it from the breakfast area, yet allowing for easy traffic flow. An alternate design is included with a master sitting room replacing the fourth bedroom.

Bentridge

FRANK BETZ ASSOCIATES, INC.

BEDROOMS 4
BATH 2-1/2
WIDTH . . . . 41'0"
DEPTH . . . . 39'4"
1ST FLOOR . . . . 947 sq ft
2ND FLOOR . . . . 981 sq ft
LIVING AREA . . . . 1928 sq ft
FOUNDATION . . . . CRAWL SPACE, SLAB
    OR BASEMENT
PLAN NUMBER **SDHFB01-3666**

REAR ELEVATION

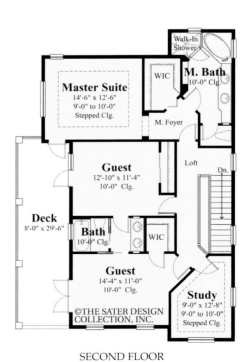

© The Sater Design Collection, In

A wraparound portico, multiple gables with decorative vents and louvered shutters garner attention from those who pass by the *Cabrini*. Inside, columns and specialty ceilings define the dining and great rooms, while multiple sets of French doors open the common living space to the outdoors. Nearby, the kitchen features a convenient pass-thru and center work island. On the upper level, the master suite and guest bedrooms enjoy privacy and access to the deck.

Cabrini

THE SATER DESIGN
COLLECTION, INC.

BEDROOMS	3
BATH	2-1/2
WIDTH	32'8"
DEPTH	72'0"
1ST FLOOR	1085 sq ft
2ND FLOOR	1093 sq ft
LIVING AREA	2178 sq ft
FOUNDATION	SLAB
PLAN NUMBER	**SDHDS01-6516**

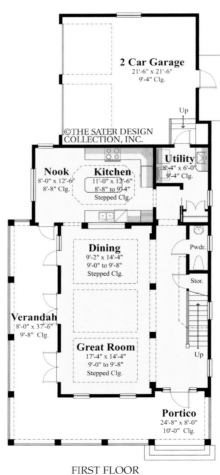

FIRST FLOOR

SECOND FLOOR

PRICING FOR SDHDG01-503

SETS	PRICE
1	$575
5	$630
8	$690
VELLUM	$960
CD	$1720

REAR ELEVATION

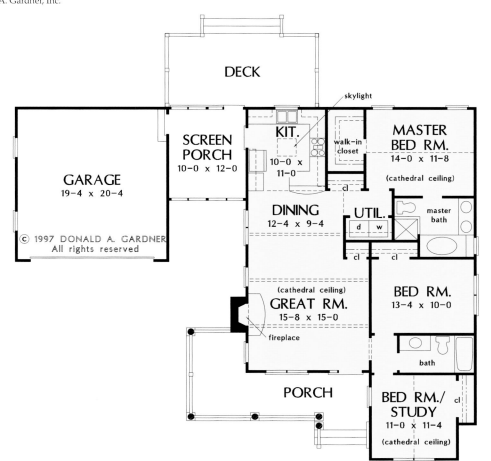

DECK

SCREEN PORCH
10-0 x 12-0

GARAGE
19-4 x 20-4

skylight

KIT.
10-0 x 11-0

walk-in closet

MASTER BED RM.
14-0 x 11-8
(cathedral ceiling)

DINING
12-4 x 9-4

UTIL.
d w

master bath

cl

(cathedral ceiling)
GREAT RM.
15-8 x 15-0

fireplace

BED RM.
13-4 x 10-0

bath

PORCH

BED RM./ STUDY
11-0 x 11-4
(cathedral ceiling)

cl

FIRST FLOOR

We created this spacious home in just 1,246 square feet by opening up the living spaces to flow into one another and vaulting the ceilings in key rooms for added volume. Two bedrooms share a bath up front, while the master suite with cathedral ceiling, walk-in closet, and well-equipped bath maintains privacy in back.

Ryley

DONALD A. GARDNER ARCHITECTS, INC.

BEDROOMS 3
BATH 2
WIDTH . . . . 60'0"
DEPTH. . . . . 48'0"
1ST FLOOR. . . . . 1246 sq ft
LIVING AREA . . . . 1246 sq ft
FOUNDATION. . . . . CRAWL SPACE*
PLAN NUMBER. **SDHDG01-503**

*Other options available. See page 175.

PRICING FOR SDHDS01-8022

SETS	PRICE
1	N/A
6	$1642
8	N/A
VELLUM	$1642
CD	$3010

© The Sater Design Collection, Inc.

REAR ELEVATION

Trefoil windows and a sculpted portico set off an Italian aesthetic inspired by 15th-century forms and an oceanfront attitude. Inside, French doors open the great room to the courtyard and terrace. A private wing that includes the kitchen and morning nook also opens to the outdoors. The master suite enjoys ample amounts of space, while the upper level harbors two guest suites, a loft and a bonus room with a bay tower.

Bartolini

THE SATER DESIGN COLLECTION, INC.

BEDROOMS 3
BATH 2-1/2
WIDTH . . . . 60'6"
DEPTH . . . . 94'0"
1ST FLOOR . . . . 2084 sq ft
2ND FLOOR . . . . 652 sq ft
LIVING AREA . . . . 2736 sq ft
BONUS ROOM . . . . 375 sq ft
FOUNDATION . . . . SLAB
PLAN NUMBER **SDHDS01-8022**

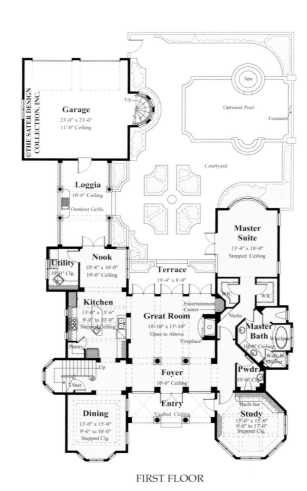

FIRST FLOOR

SECOND FLOOR

PRICING FOR
SDHDG01-993

SETS	PRICE
1	$620
5	$680
8	$730
VELLUM	$1025
CD	$1850

REAR ELEVATION

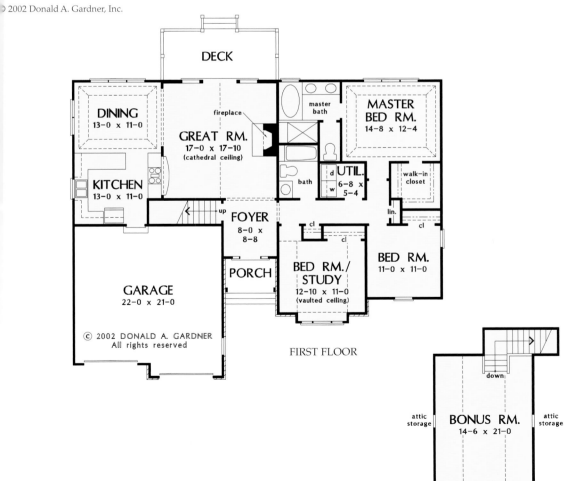

DECK

DINING
13-0 x 11-0

fireplace

GREAT RM.
17-0 x 17-10
(cathedral ceiling)

master
bath

MASTER
BED RM.
14-8 x 12-4

KITCHEN
13-0 x 11-0

bath

d UTIL.
w 6-8 x
5-4

walk-in
closet

up

FOYER
8-0 x
8-8

lin.

BED RM./
STUDY
12-10 x 11-0
(vaulted ceiling)

BED RM.
11-0 x 11-0

PORCH

GARAGE
22-0 x 21-0

FIRST FLOOR

down

attic
storage

BONUS RM.
14-6 x 21-0

attic
storage

This cottage combines stone and siding
for a striking façade. A box-bay window
is capped with a metal roof, while the
front-entry garage adds convenience.
Decorative ceiling treatments enhance
the great room, dining room, master
bedroom and the study/bedroom. The
bonus room, which is accessible from the
foyer, provides space for a home office,
gym or media room.

Irby

DONALD A. GARDNER
ARCHITECTS, INC.

BEDROOMS 3
BATH 2
WIDTH . . . . 55'6"
DEPTH . . . . 46'0"
1ST FLOOR . . . . 1580 sq ft
LIVING AREA . . . . 1580 sq ft
BONUS ROOM . . . . 367 sq ft
FOUNDATION . . . . CRAWL SPACE*
PLAN NUMBER **SDHDG01-993**

*Other options available. See page 175.

PRICING FOR
SDHDG01-1027

SETS	PRICE
1	$620
5	$680
8	$730
VELLUM	$1025
CD	$1850

REAR ELEVATION

With a hint of Old-World style, this cottage showcases a beautiful mixture of stone, siding and architectural detail. Front and rear porches expand living outdoors, while a side porch creates a service entrance into the utility/mudroom. A vaulted ceiling highlights the dining room, and a smart, angled counter separates the kitchen from the breakfast nook and great room.

Bookworth

DONALD A. GARDNER ARCHITECTS, INC.

BEDROOMS 3
BATH 2
WIDTH . . . . 61'10"
DEPTH. . . . . 62'6"
1ST FLOOR . . . . 1820 sq ft
LIVING AREA . . . . 1820 sq ft
FOUNDATION. . . . . CRAWL SPACE*
PLAN NUMBER. **SDHDG01-1027**

*Other options available. See page 175.

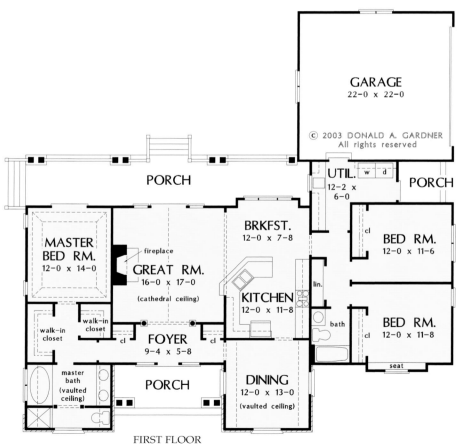

GARAGE
22-0 x 22-0

PORCH

UTIL.
12-2 x 6-0

PORCH

BRKFST.
12-0 x 7-8

BED RM.
12-0 x 11-6

MASTER BED RM.
12-0 x 14-0

fireplace

GREAT RM.
16-0 x 17-0
(cathedral ceiling)

KITCHEN
12-0 x 11-8

lin.

bath

walk-in closet

walk-in closet

cl

FOYER
9-4 x 5-8

cl

BED RM.
12-0 x 11-8

seat

master bath
(vaulted ceiling)

PORCH

DINING
12-0 x 13-0
(vaulted ceiling)

FIRST FLOOR

PRICING FOR SDHGA01-07252

SETS	PRICE
1	N/A
5	$1595
8	N/A
VELLUM	$1695
CD	$2645

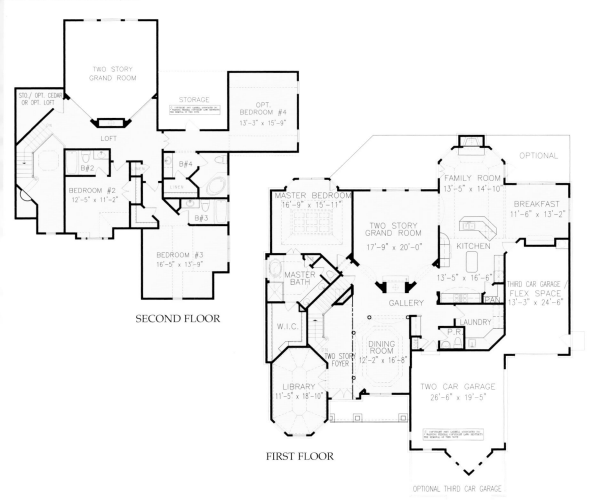

SECOND FLOOR

FIRST FLOOR

OPTIONAL THIRD CAR GARAGE

REAR ELEVATION

Reminiscent of an English cottage, the *Heatherton* has a stone and shake façade giving it a warm curb appeal. The foyer opens to a spacious formal dining area and large library with double doors. A master suite on the main floor offers privacy, while three additional bedroom suites on the second floor are perfect for a growing family.

Heatherton-3183

GARRELL ASSOCIATES, INC.

BEDROOMS 3
BATH 3-1/2
WIDTH . . . . 63'6"
DEPTH . . . . 88'2"
1ST FLOOR . . . . 2493 sq ft
2ND FLOOR . . . . 690 sq ft
LIVING AREA . . . . 3183 sq ft
BONUS ROOM . . . . 471 sq ft
FOUNDATION . . . . BASEMENT
PLAN NUMBER SDHGA01-07252

PRICING FOR
SDHFB01-3551

SETS	PRICE
1	$870
5	$920
8	$970
VELLUM	$1190
CD	$2065

REAR ELEVATION

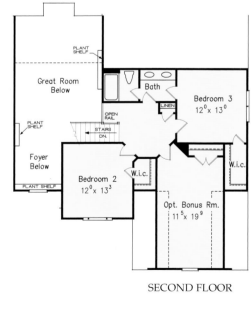

A distinctive turret with arched windows is the focal point of the façade on the *Ambrose*. A covered entry leads to an interesting and thoughtful layout inside. Family time is well spent in the large sunroom, situated just beyond the breakfast area. The bedroom on the main level easily transforms into a home office — perfect for the telecommuter or retiree.

Ambrose

FRANK BETZ ASSOCIATES, INC.

BEDROOMS 4
BATH 3
WIDTH . . . . 54'0"
DEPTH . . . . 60'0"
1ST FLOOR . . . . 2003 sq ft
2ND FLOOR . . . . 579 sq ft
LIVING AREA . . . . 2582 sq ft
OPT. BONUS ROOM . . . 262 sq ft
FOUNDATION . . . . CRAWL SPACE, SLAB OR BASEMENT
PLAN NUMBER **SDHFB01-3551**

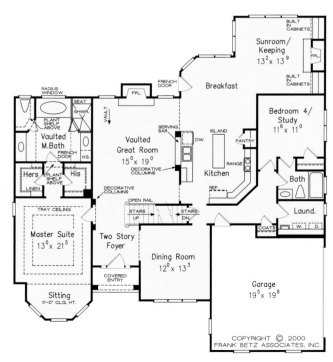

FIRST FLOOR

SECOND FLOOR

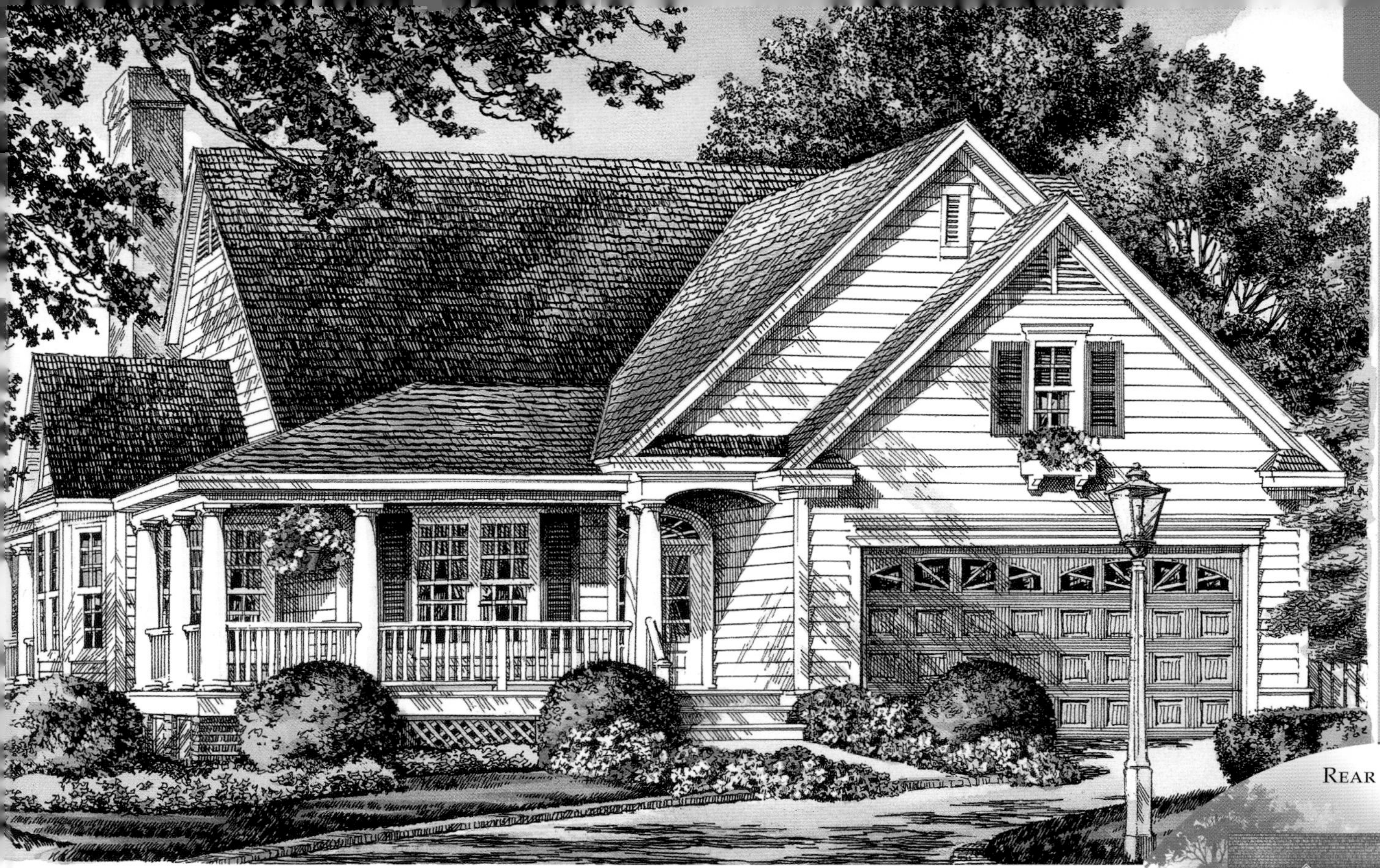

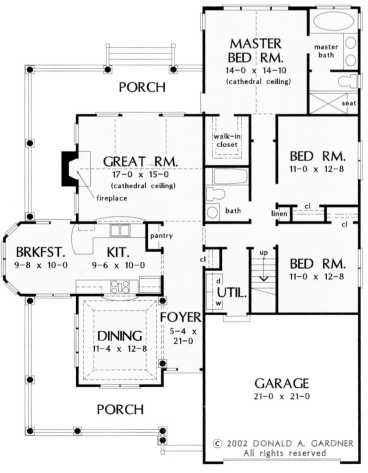

PRICING FOR SDHDG01-983

Sets	Price
1	$620
5	$680
8	$730
VELLUM	$1025
CD	$1850

Rear Elevation

MASTER BED RM.
14-0 x 14-10
(cathedral ceiling)
master bath
seat
PORCH
walk-in closet
GREAT RM.
17-0 x 15-0
(cathedral ceiling)
fireplace
BED RM.
11-0 x 12-8
bath
linen
cl
cl
pantry
BRKFST.
9-8 x 10-0
KIT.
9-6 x 10-0
cl
up
d
UTIL.
w
BED RM.
11-0 x 12-8
FOYER
5-4 x 21-0
DINING
11-4 x 12-8
GARAGE
21-0 x 21-0
PORCH
© 2002 DONALD A. GARDNER
All rights reserved

FIRST FLOOR

down
attic storage
attic storage
BONUS RM.
13-4 x 21-0

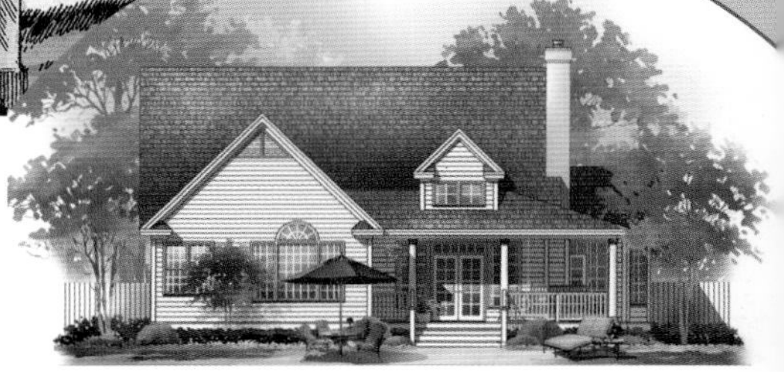

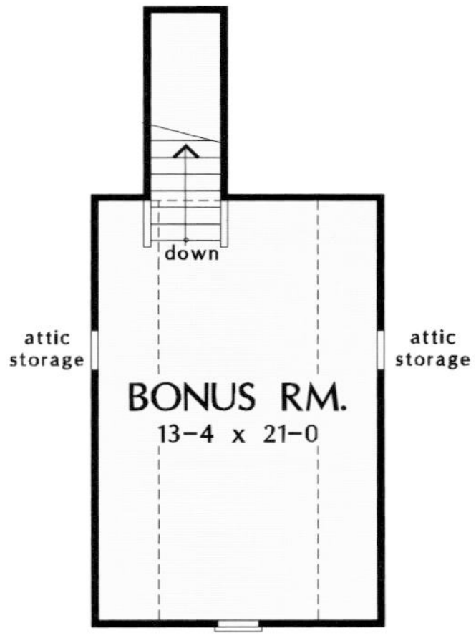

An abundance of windows invite the natural surroundings inside, while two gracious porches create spaces for outdoor living. Custom-styled features include a tray ceiling in the dining room, cathedral ceilings in the great room and master bedroom, and French doors that lead to the rear porch. The kitchen includes two handy pass-thrus, and columns mark entry to the dining room.

Jonesboro

DONALD A. GARDNER ARCHITECTS, INC.

BEDROOMS 3
BATH 2
WIDTH .... 49'0"
DEPTH............... 65'4"
1ST FLOOR........... 1700 sq ft
LIVING AREA .... 1700 sq ft
BONUS ROOM......... 333 sq ft
FOUNDATION......... CRAWL SPACE*
PLAN NUMBER...... SDHDG01-983

*Other options available. See page 175.

© 2005 Frank Betz Associates, In

PRICING FOR
SDHFB01-3936

SETS	PRICE
1	$810
5	$860
8	$910
VELLUM	$1095
CD	$1895

REAR ELEVATION

One-level ranch plans are as popular as ever, and the *Kingsbridge* is no exception. This plan was designed for an easy flow through the home. The master bedroom is on one wing while the secondary bedrooms are on the other side. An additional bonus room or bedroom is on the optional second floor, making future expansion a possibility.

Kingsbridge

FRANK BETZ ASSOCIATES, INC.

BEDROOMS 3
BATH 3-1/2
WIDTH . . . . 59'4"
DEPTH. . . . . 70'0"
1ST FLOOR. . . . . 2289 sq ft
LIVING AREA . . . . 2289 sq ft
OPT. 2ND FLOOR. . . . . 311 sq ft
FOUNDATION. . . . . CRAWL SPACE, SLAB OR BASEMENT
PLAN NUMBER **SDHFB01-3936**

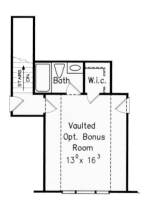

OPT. SECOND FLOOR

FIRST FLOOR

COPYRIGHT © 2005
FRANK BETZ ASSOCIATES, INC.

PRICING FOR SDHDS01-6785

SETS	PRICE
1	N/A
6	$1526
8	N/A
VELLUM	$1526
CD	$2798

REAR ELEVATION

FIRST FLOOR

Floor plan labels:

- Bath 3
- Entertainment Center
- Leisure Room — 17'-3" x 15'-8" — 10'-0" to 11'-0" — Stepped Clg.
- Nook — 5'-6" x 8'-6" — 10'-0" Clg.
- Lanai — 26'-2" x 9'-4" — 10'-0" Clg.
- Bedroom 4 — 11'-8" x 11'-0" — 10'-0" Clg.
- Kitchen — 10'-0" to 11'-0" — Stepped Clg.
- Living Room — 16'-3" x 15'-2" — 12'-0" to 13'-0" — Stepped Clg.
- Master Suite — 16'-7" x 14'-0" — 10'-0" to 12'-0" — Tray Clg.
- Bedroom 3 — 11'-0" x 11'-0" — 10'-0" Clg.
- Pantry
- Art Niches
- Bath 2
- Niche
- Arch
- W.I.C.
- Bedroom 2 — 11'-8" x 13'-4" — 10'-0" Clg.
- Utility — 10'-0" Clg.
- Dining Room — 11'-8" x 10'-2" — 11'-0" to 12'-0" — Stepped Clg.
- Foyer
- Entry
- Master Bath — 9'-0" x 15'-2" — 10'-0" Clg.
- Built-ins
- Storage
- Garage — 20'-8" x 24'-2" — 11'-4" Clg.

Decorative pendants add one-of-a-kind detail to the entryway cornice. Inside, the living room, kitchen and leisure room flow together and offer uninterrupted access and views to the lanai through disappearing glass walls and mitered windows. An island and large walk-in pantry make the kitchen sparkle. Owners will enjoy privacy in a master suite tucked to one side of the home.

La Posada

THE SATER DESIGN COLLECTION, INC.

BEDROOMS 4
BATH 3
WIDTH . . . . 60'4"
DEPTH . . . . 78'9"
1ST FLOOR . . . . 2544 sq ft
LIVING AREA . . . . 2544 sq ft
FOUNDATION . . . . SLAB
PLAN NUMBER SDHDS01-6785

PRICING FOR SDHDG01-1008

SETS	PRICE
1	$665
5	$725
8	$775
VELLUM	$1090
CD	$1980

REAR ELEVATION

Low-maintenance siding, a convenient front-entry garage and architectural details such as gables and half-circle transoms make this narrow-lot charmer perfect for beginning families and empty nesters. Custom-styled features include a plant shelf in the foyer, fireplace, two-story great room ceiling, kitchen pass-thru and French doors leading to the rear porch.

Dayton

DONALD A. GARDNER ARCHITECTS, INC.

BEDROOMS 3
BATH 2-1/2
WIDTH . . . . 47'0"
DEPTH . . . . 55'0"
1ST FLOOR . . . . 1569 sq ft
2ND FLOOR . . . . 504 sq ft
LIVING AREA . . . . 2073 sq ft
BONUS ROOM . . . . 320 sq ft
FOUNDATION . . . . CRAWL SPACE*
PLAN NUMBER **SDHDG01-1008**

*Other options available. See page 175.

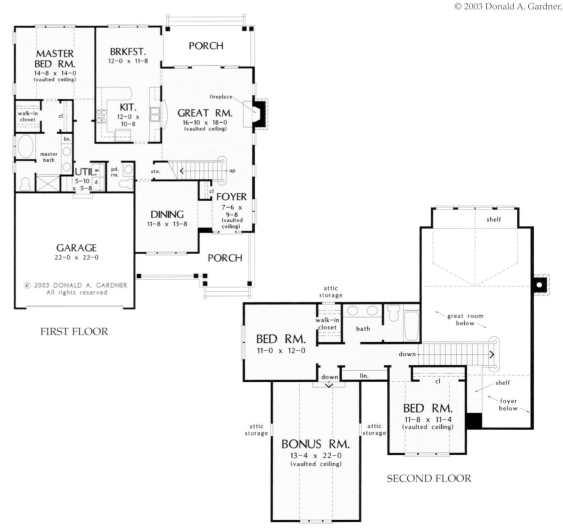

FIRST FLOOR

SECOND FLOOR

PRICING FOR SDHFB01-3828

SETS	PRICE
1	$810
5	$860
8	$910
VELLUM	$1095
CD	$1895

REAR ELEVATION

Beamed gables and cedar shake create an appealing Craftsman-style elevation on the *Camden Lake*. Double ovens, a serving bar and a liberally sized pantry make the kitchen a user-friendly room. Its view to the cozy keeping room warms the entire space, creating an inviting environment.

Camden Lake

FRANK BETZ ASSOCIATES, INC.

BEDROOMS 4
BATH 3-1/2
WIDTH . . . . 62'6"
DEPTH . . . . 77'4"
1ST FLOOR . . . . 2395 sq ft
LIVING AREA . . . . 2395 sq ft
OPT. 2ND FLOOR . . . . . 660 sq ft
FOUNDATION . . . . CRAWL SPACE, SLAB OR BASEMENT
PLAN NUMBER **SDHFB01-3828**

FIRST FLOOR

OPT. SECOND FLOOR

REAR ELEVATION

© 2004 Frank Betz Associates, Inc.

Timber-accented gables and hearty fieldstone give the *Culbertson* a personality all its own. The kitchen overlooks a keeping room with a fireplace, giving families a cozy place to gather for a board game. A screened porch adjoins the kitchen area, extending the space for outdoor entertaining.

Culbertson

FRANK BETZ ASSOCIATES, INC.

BEDROOMS 4
BATH 2-1/2
WIDTH . . . . 52'4"
DEPTH . . . . 55'10"
1ST FLOOR . . . . 1214 sq ft
2ND FLOOR . . . . 1229 sq ft
LIVING AREA . . . . 2443 sq ft
FOUNDATION . . . . CRAWL SPACE, SLAB OR BASEMENT
PLAN NUMBER **SDHFB01-3860**

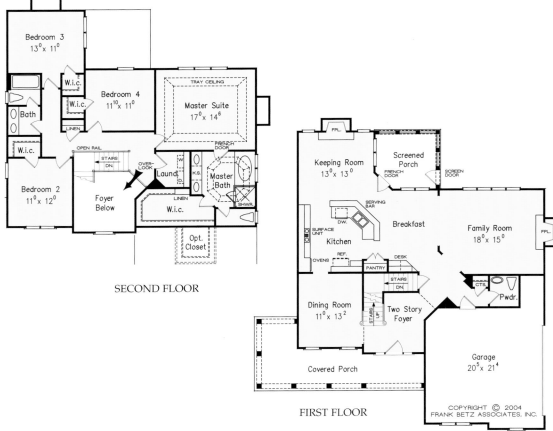

SECOND FLOOR

FIRST FLOOR

PRICING FOR SDHDG01-290

SETS	PRICE
1	$665
5	$725
8	$775
VELLUM	$1090
CD	$1980

FIRST FLOOR

DECK

spa

seat · seat

SCREENED PORCH
15-4 x 10-0

PORCH

up · storage

GARAGE
22-4 x 25-8

BRKFST.
10-8 x 9-0

UTILITY
7-8 x 9-4

d w

covered breezeway

GREAT RM.
17-4 x 19-4
(sloped ceiling)

fireplace

cabinets

balcony above

MASTER BED RM.
16-8 x 15-6

KITCHEN
12-8 x 12-8

cl

walk-in closet

lin.

master bath

sto.

cl

pd. rm.

DINING
15-0 x 12-4

FOYER
11-8 x 7-0

up

PORCH

SECOND FLOOR

clerestory with palladian window

attic storage

great room below

attic storage

railing

BED RM.
12-8 x 12-0

balcony

BED RM.
12-8 x 12-0

down

bath

cl

cl

cl

cl

foyer below

clerestory with palladian window

BONUS RM.
15-4 x 25-8

down

A two-story great room and two-story foyer, both with dormer windows, welcome natural light into this graceful country classic with wraparound porch. The large kitchen, featuring a central cooktop island with serving counter and a large breakfast bay, opens to the great room for easy entertaining. Columns punctuate the interior spaces, and the semi-detached garage features a large bonus room.

REAR ELEVATION

Burgess

DONALD A. GARDNER ARCHITECTS, INC.

BEDROOMS 3
BATH 2-1/2
WIDTH . . . . 54'0"
DEPTH . . . . 57'0"
1ST FLOOR . . . . 1618 sq ft
2ND FLOOR . . . . 570 sq ft
LIVING AREA . . . . 2188 sq ft
BONUS ROOM . . . . 495 sq ft
FOUNDATION . . . . CRAWL SPACE*
PLAN NUMBER **SDHDG01-290**

*Other options available. See page 175.

SETS	PRICE
1	$870
5	$920
8	$970
VELLUM	$1190
CD	$2065

REAR ELEVATION

© 1998 Frank Betz Associates, I

The *Sullivan's* full brick façade, as well as the classic turret, has stood the test of time. The home is anchored by a vaulted great room that adjoins the kitchen and breakfast areas — a perfect layout for entertaining. The master suite is private and well-appointed, complete with his-and- her closets, a lavish bath and comfortable sitting area.

Sullivan

FRANK BETZ ASSOCIATES, INC.

BEDROOMS	4
BATH	3
WIDTH	54'0"
DEPTH	48'0"
1ST FLOOR	1688 sq ft
2ND FLOOR	558 sq ft
LIVING AREA	2246 sq ft
OPT. BONUS ROOM	269 sq ft
FOUNDATION	CRAWL SPACE, SLAB OR BASEMENT
PLAN NUMBER	SDHFB01-1224

FIRST FLOOR

COPYRIGHT © 1998
FRANK BETZ ASSOCIATES, INC.

SECOND FLOOR

PRICING FOR SDHDS01-7078

SETS	PRICE
1	N/A
6	$1742
8	N/A
VELLUM	$1742
CD	$3194

REAR VIEW

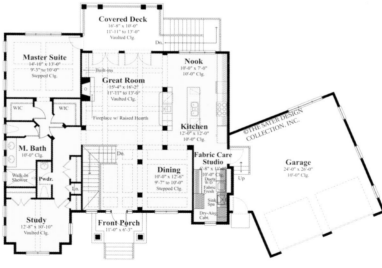

FIRST FLOOR

BASEMENT

This contemporary Arts-and-Crafts home celebrates the outdoors with a floor plan that provides smart transitions between public and private realms while keeping the wide-open views in mind. Inside, columns and a tray ceiling define the formal dining room. Nearby is the home's centerpiece, the impressive great room. As grand as it is cozy, it features a fireplace, built-in cabinetry and glass doors providing a seamless connection to the outdoors.

Dune Ridge

THE SATER DESIGN COLLECTION, INC.

BEDROOMS 3
BATH 2-1/2
WIDTH . . . . 76'8"
DEPTH. . . . . 52'11"
1ST FLOOR. . . . . 1711 sq ft
BASEMENT . . . . 1193 sq ft
LIVING AREA . . . . 2904 sq ft
FOUNDATION. . . . . HILLSIDE WALKOUT
PLAN NUMBER. **SDHDS01-7078**

© 2001-2007 Garrell Associates, Inc

PRICING FOR
SDHGA01-01049

SETS	PRICE
1	N/A
5	$1665
8	N/A
VELLUM	$1765
CD	$2715

REAR ELEVATION

Elegant style in stone and shake describe this warm family home. The master suite with a sitting room and optional fireplace on the main floor offers a quiet retreat for the homeowner . An angled keeping room, gourmet kitchen and morning room provide a spacious gathering area for family and friends. Three generous suites on the second level complete this gracious home.

Tres Maison

GARRELL
ASSOCIATES, INC.

BEDROOMS 4
BATH 3-1/2
WIDTH . . . . 68'11"
DEPTH. . . . . 65'9"
1ST FLOOR. . . . . 2523 sq ft
2ND FLOOR. . . . . 870 sq ft
LIVING AREA . . . . 3393 sq ft
FOUNDATION. . . . . . . BASEMENT
PLAN NUMBER. **SDHGA01-01049**

FIRST FLOOR

SECOND FLOOR

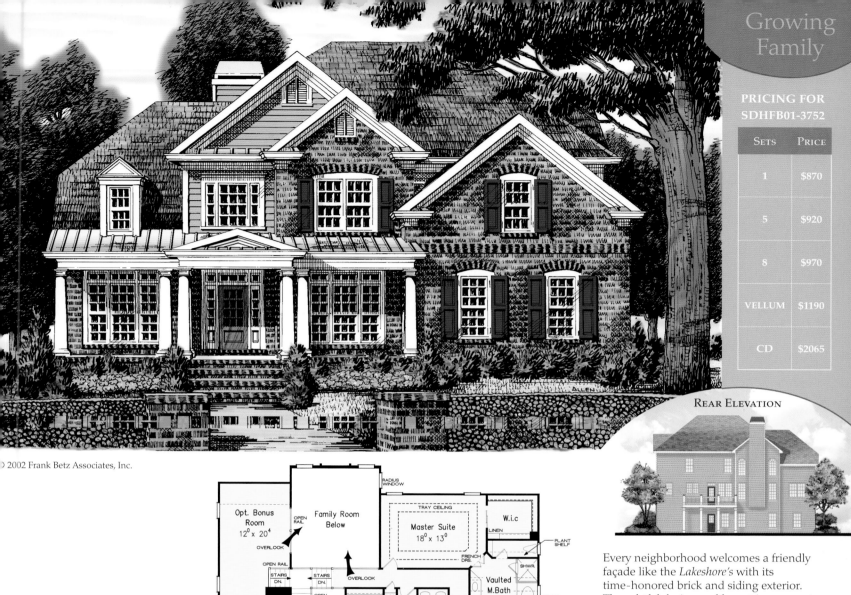

© 2002 Frank Betz Associates, Inc.

**PRICING FOR
SDHFB01-3752**

SETS	PRICE
1	$870
5	$920
8	$970
VELLUM	$1190
CD	$2065

REAR ELEVATION

SECOND FLOOR

- Opt. Bonus Room 12⁰ x 20⁴
- OVERLOOK
- OPEN RAIL
- Family Room Below
- RADIUS WINDOW
- OPEN RAIL
- TRAY CEILING
- Master Suite 18⁰ x 13⁰
- W.i.c
- LINEN
- PLANT SHELF
- FRENCH DRS.
- SHWR.
- STAIRS DN.
- STAIRS DN.
- OVERLOOK
- OPEN RAIL
- Foyer Below
- LN.
- Bedroom 2 12⁰ x 13⁴
- Vaulted M.Bath
- K.S.
- RADIUS WINDOW
- Bath
- Bedroom 3 11² x 13⁵
- W.i.c.

FIRST FLOOR

- FPL.
- Bedroom 4/ Den 12⁰ x 11²
- Two Story Family Room 15⁰ x 18⁰
- FRENCH DOOR
- D.W.
- Breakfast
- ISLAND
- REF.
- Kitchen
- SURF. UNIT OVENS
- W.
- D.
- Laun.
- PANTRY
- W.i.c.
- Bath
- LINEN
- STAIRS DN.
- COATS
- BUTLERS PANTRY
- Vaulted Living Room 12⁰ x 12³
- STAIRS UP
- Two Story Foyer
- Dining Room 12⁰ x 13⁴
- Garage 20⁵ x 22²
- Covered Porch
- COPYRIGHT © 2002 FRANK BETZ ASSOCIATES, INC.

Every neighborhood welcomes a friendly façade like the *Lakeshore's* with its time-honored brick and siding exterior. Thoughtful design and layout is apparent inside. A large island, double ovens and a butler's pantry take the work out of entertaining. Its master suite features a large private bath, a generous walk-in closet and views to the backyard.

Lakeshore

FRANK BETZ ASSOCIATES, INC.

BEDROOMS 4
BATH 3
WIDTH . . . . 55'0"
DEPTH . . . . 47'10"
1ST FLOOR . . . . 1483 sq ft
2ND FLOOR . . . . 1024 sq ft
LIVING AREA . . . . 2507 sq ft
OPT. BONUS ROOM . . . 252 sq ft
FOUNDATION . . . . CRAWL SPACE
OR BASEMENT
PLAN NUMBER **SDHFB01-3752**

PRICING FOR
SDHDG01-970

SETS	PRICE
1	$620
5	$680
8	$730
VELLUM	$1025
CD	$1850

REAR ELEVATION

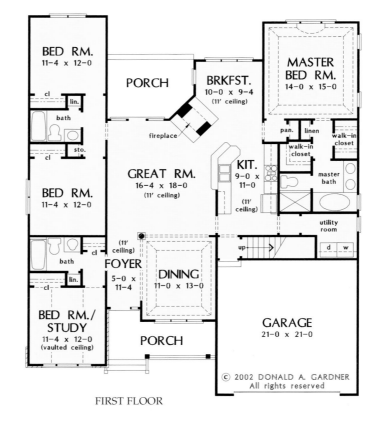

As at home in a development as it is on an orchard, this design combines country charm with Craftsman appeal. A sole column and tray ceiling distinguish the dining room that opens to a great room. With a master bath, two full additional baths, an optional study/bedroom, and bonus room, this home has plenty of space for growing families.

Applemoor

DONALD A. GARDNER ARCHITECTS, INC.

BEDROOMS 4
BATH 3
WIDTH . . . . 50'0"
DEPTH. . . . . 60'0"
1ST FLOOR. . . . . 1952 sq ft
LIVING AREA . . . . 1952 sq ft
BONUS ROOM. . . . . . . 339 sq ft
FOUNDATION. . . . . CRAWL SPACE*
PLAN NUMBER. **SDHDG01-970**

FIRST FLOOR

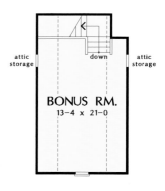

*Other options available. See page 175.

2002 Visbeen Associates, Inc.

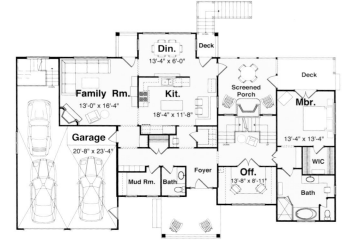

FIRST FLOOR

REAR ELEVATION

Filled with both comfort and charm, this classic all-American home features a welcoming farmhouse flavor. A large open, main-floor plan includes a spacious kitchen with a cozy eating nook, a family room with a fireplace and beamed ceiling, a handy office and mudroom and a private master bedroom suite. Upstairs are three additional bedrooms, while the lower level features a family room with kitchenette and an additional guest bedroom.

Brighton

VISBEEN ASSOCIATES, INC.

BEDROOMS	5
BATH	4
WIDTH	75'0"
DEPTH	48'0"
1ST FLOOR	1864 sq ft
2ND FLOOR	855 sq ft
LIVING AREA	2719 sq ft
OPT. BASEMENT	1012 sq ft
FOUNDATION	WALKOUT
PLAN NUMBER	**SDHVA01-9029**

OPT. BASEMENT

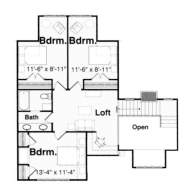

SECOND FLOOR

PRICING FOR SDHDG01-960

SETS	PRICE
1	$665
5	$725
8	$775
VELLUM	$1090
CD	$1980

REAR ELEVATION

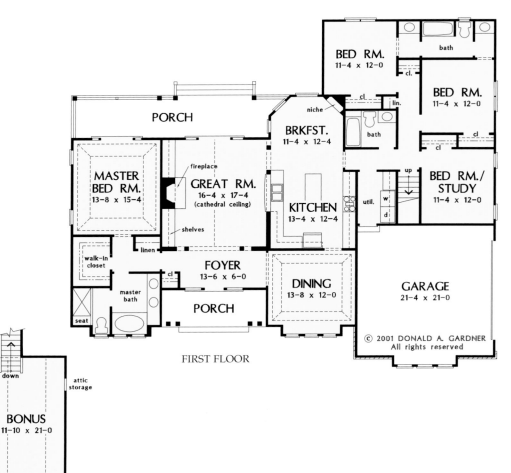

Built-ins, a vaulted ceiling and a fireplace highlight the great room, which is connected to the kitchen by a pass-thru. Tray ceilings crown both the dining room and master bedroom, while French doors in the master bedroom and great room lead to the rear porch. A study/bedroom and bonus room allow versatility, and the master suite is located for privacy.

Xavier

DONALD A. GARDNER ARCHITECTS, INC.

BEDROOMS 4
BATH 3
WIDTH . . . . 66'8"
DEPTH. . . . . 56'6"
1ST FLOOR. . . . . 2174 sq ft
LIVING AREA . . . . 2174 sq ft
BONUS ROOM. . . . . . . 299 sq ft
FOUNDATION. . . . . CRAWL SPACE*
PLAN NUMBER **SDHDG01-960**

*Other options available. See page 175.

Floor plan labels:

PORCH

BED RM.
11-4 x 12-0
bath
cl.

BED RM.
11-4 x 12-0
cl.

niche
BRKFST.
11-4 x 12-4
cl. lin.
bath

MASTER BED RM.
13-8 x 15-4
fireplace
GREAT RM.
16-4 x 17-4
(cathedral ceiling)
shelves
KITCHEN
13-4 x 12-4
util.
w
d
up

BED RM./ STUDY
11-4 x 12-0

walk-in closet
linen
cl

master bath
seat
cl
FOYER
13-6 x 6-0

DINING
13-8 x 12-0

GARAGE
21-4 x 21-0

PORCH

FIRST FLOOR

attic storage
down
attic storage

BONUS
11-10 x 21-0

PRICING FOR SDHFB01-3712

SETS	PRICE
1	$810
5	$860
8	$910
VELLUM	$1095
CD	$1895

REAR ELEVATION

Tradition is appreciated in the thoughtful design of *Defoors Mill*. The master suite encompasses an entire wing of the home for comfort and privacy. Special details in this home include a handy island in the kitchen, decorative columns around the dining area and a coat closet just off the garage.

FIRST FLOOR

COPYRIGHT © 2002
FRANK BETZ ASSOCIATES, INC.

SECOND FLOOR

Defoors Mill

FRANK BETZ ASSOCIATES, INC.

BEDROOMS 4
BATH 3
WIDTH . . . . 55'0"
DEPTH . . . . 48'0"
1ST FLOOR . . . . 1803 sq ft
2ND FLOOR . . . . 548 sq ft
LIVING AREA . . . . 2351 sq ft
OPT. BONUS ROOM . . . 277 sq ft
FOUNDATION . . . . CRAWL SPACE, SLAB
OR BASEMENT
PLAN NUMBER **SDHFB01-3712**

PRICING FOR SDHDS01-6688

SETS	PRICE
1	N/A
6	$1724
8	N/A
VELLUM	$1724
CD	$3160

REAR VIEW

© The Sater Design Collection, Inc

A Charleston Row courtyard complete with a sundeck, spa and lap pool make this villa a relaxing retreat. Inside, arches and columns provide definition to the kitchen, dining and great rooms. French doors extend the living areas to the covered porch. The second level includes two guest bedrooms and the master suite. A bonus room over the garage offers many options.

Wulfert Point

THE SATER DESIGN COLLECTION, INC.

BEDROOMS 4
BATH 3-1/2
WIDTH . . . . 50'0"
DEPTH . . . . 90'0"
1ST FLOOR . . . . 1293 sq ft
2ND FLOOR . . . . 1154 sq ft
LIVING AREA . . . . 2873 sq ft
FOUNDATION . . . . SLAB
PLAN NUMBER **SDHDS01-6688**

FIRST FLOOR

SECOND FLOOR

©THE SATER DESIGN COLLECTION, INC.

PRICING FOR SDHDG01-715

SETS	PRICE
1	$620
5	$680
8	$730
VELLUM	$1025
CD	$1850

REAR ELEVATION

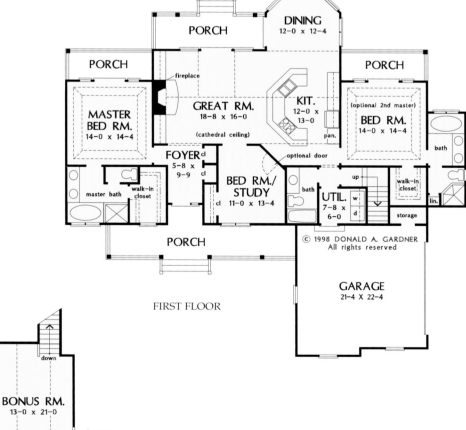

FIRST FLOOR

DINING
12-0 x 12-4

PORCH

PORCH

PORCH

fireplace

GREAT RM.
18-8 x 16-0
(cathedral ceiling)

KIT.
12-0 x 13-0

pan.

(optional 2nd master)

BED RM.
14-0 x 14-4

bath

MASTER BED RM.
14-0 x 14-4

FOYER
5-8 x 9-9

cl

cl

optional door

master bath

walk-in closet

BED RM./STUDY
11-0 x 13-4

cl

bath

UTIL.
7-8 x 6-0

w d

up

walk-in closet

lin.

storage

© 1998 DONALD A. GARDNER
All rights reserved

PORCH

GARAGE
21-4 X 22-4

BONUS RM.
13-0 x 21-0

down

attic storage

attic storage

Cedar shakes and siding create a custom look for this Craftsman home. With three porches and a surplus of windows across the back, this home takes advantage of exceptional rear views. The great room, kitchen and dining room are open, combining as a spacious common area. For added volume, a cathedral ceiling caps both the great room and kitchen.

Larkspur

DONALD A. GARDNER ARCHITECTS, INC.

BEDROOMS 3
BATH 3
WIDTH . . . . 66'4"
DEPTH. . . . . 62'4"
1ST FLOOR. . . . . 1792 sq ft
LIVING AREA . . . . 1792 sq ft
BONUS ROOM. . . . . . . 338 sq ft
FOUNDATION. . . . . . . CRAWL SPACE*
PLAN NUMBER. **SDHDG01-715**

*Other options available. See page 175.

PRICING FOR SDHDG01-896

SETS	PRICE
1	$620
5	$680
8	$730
VELLUM	$1025
CD	$1850

REAR ELEVATION

Larger plans have nothing on this home; it's designed to indulge. Magnificent treatments such as a cathedral ceiling in the great room, tray ceiling in the dining room and vaulted ceiling in a secondary bedroom add volume, while the fireplace is bordered by built-ins. An angled counter separates the kitchen from the great room and breakfast area without enclosing space.

Fenmore

DONALD A. GARDNER ARCHITECTS, INC.

BEDROOMS 3
BATH 2
WIDTH . . . . 50'0"
DEPTH . . . . 54'0"
1ST FLOOR . . . . 1593 sq ft
LIVING AREA . . . . 1593 sq ft
BONUS ROOM . . . . 332 sq ft
FOUNDATION . . . . CRAWL SPACE*
PLAN NUMBER **SDHDG01-896**

*Other options available. See page 175.

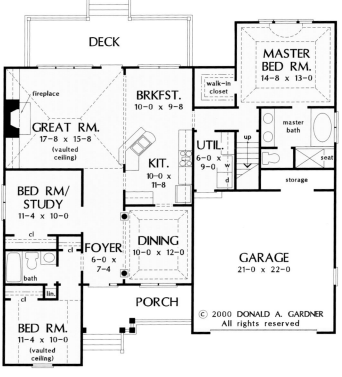

FIRST FLOOR

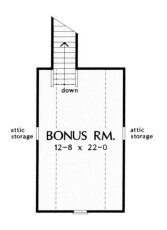

The Sater Design Collection, Inc.

REAR ELEVATION

FIRST FLOOR

SECOND FLOOR

LOWER LEVEL

A double-stepped staircase and a curved balcony complement the arched entryway of this coastal home. Inside, the foyer embraces the living areas accented by a three-sided fireplace and wet bar. Sliding glass doors bring views in to the open rooms and provide access to the verandah. Nearby, the kitchen features a breakfast nook and easily interacts with the verandah for outdoor entertaining. Upstairs, the master suite enjoys a sundeck and three-sided fireplace.

Galleon Bay

THE SATER DESIGN COLLECTION, INC.

BEDROOMS 3
BATH 3-1/2
WIDTH . . . . 64'0"
DEPTH . . . . 45'0"
1ST FLOOR . . . . 2066 sq ft
2ND FLOOR . . . . 809 sq ft
LIVING AREA . . . . 2875 sq ft
FOUNDATION . . . . ISLAND BASEMENT
PLAN NUMBER **SDHDS01-6620**

PRICING FOR SDHDG01-265

Sets	Price
1	$575
5	$630
8	$685
VELLUM	$960
CD	$1720

REAR ELEVATION

The heart of this home is the common great room, kitchen and dining area, which provides exceptional openness for visual interaction. Cathedral ceilings and built-in shelves and cabinets on either side of the fireplace add to the excitement. The spacious kitchen features an angled cooktop island with breakfast bar.

Hawthorne

DONALD A. GARDNER ARCHITECTS, INC.

BEDROOMS 3
BATH 2
WIDTH . . . . 66'4"
DEPTH. . . . . 36'0"
1ST FLOOR. . . . . 1287 sq ft
LIVING AREA . . . . 1287 sq ft
FOUNDATION. . . . . . . CRAWL SPACE*
PLAN NUMBER. **SDHDG01-265**

*Other options available. See page 175.

PRICING FOR SDHFB01-3823

SETS	PRICE
1	$870
5	$920
8	$970
VELLUM	$1190
CD	$2065

REAR ELEVATION

© 2003 Frank Betz Associates, Inc.

FIRST FLOOR

- master bedroom 13'5"× 19'0"
- family room 19'0"× 16'5"
- breakfast 12'9"× 10'3"
- screened porch 12'10"× 13'0"
- deck
- kitchen 12'5"× 12'0"
- up
- dn.
- foyer
- dining 12'0"× 12'9"
- garage 21'5"× 21'0"
- covered porch

COPYRIGHT © 2003 FRANK BETZ ASSOCIATES, INC.

SECOND FLOOR

- open to below
- bedroom 12'5"× 13'3"
- dn.
- bedroom 12'6"× 12'9"
- computer loft 16'0"× 10'0"
- opt. bonus room 16'5"× 14'10"

FROM THE Southern Living DESIGN COLLECTION

Charm and character exude from the exterior of *Catawba Ridge* with its thoughtful welcoming of stone and cedar shake. Its kitchen, breakfast area and family room are conveniently grouped together for easy family interaction. Kids will love having their own computer loft upstairs. A bonus room upstairs is ready to finish as you wish.

Catawba Ridge

FRANK BETZ ASSOCIATES, INC.

BEDROOMS 3
BATH 3-1/2
WIDTH . . . . 59'8"
DEPTH. . . . . 50'6"
1ST FLOOR. . . . . 1593 sq ft
2ND FLOOR. . . . . 796 sq ft
LIVING AREA . . . . 2389 sq ft
OPT. BONUS ROOM. . . 238 sq ft
FOUNDATION. . . . . CRAWL SPACE, SLAB OR BASEMENT
PLAN NUMBER. **SDHFB01-3823**

PRICING FOR
SDHGA01-03220

Sets	Price
1	N/A
5	$1041
8	N/A
VELLUM	$1141
CD	$1991

Rear Elevation

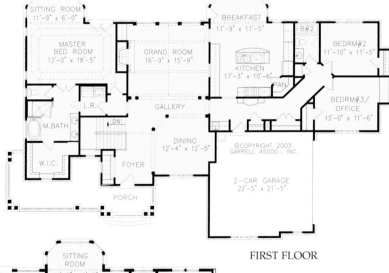

This ranch-style home features a split bedroom floor plan with spacious common areas. Many windows provide warmth and natural light throughout this beautiful home. An optional full basement plan allows for ample storage and room to grow.

Farrington Cottage

GARRELL ASSOCIATES, INC.

BEDROOMS 3
BATH 2
WIDTH . . . . 79'8"
DEPTH . . . . 52'6"
1ST FLOOR . . . . 2282 sq ft
LIVING AREA . . . . 2282 sq ft
OPT. TERRACE . . . . 2184 sq ft
FOUNDATION . . . . CRAWL SPACE, SLAB
        OR BASEMENT
PLAN NUMBER **SDHGA01-03220**

FIRST FLOOR

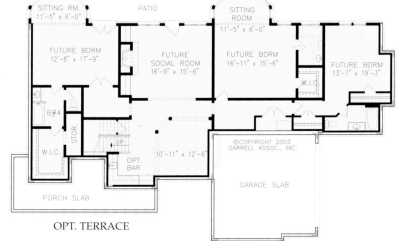

OPT. TERRACE

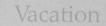

PRICING FOR SDHFB01-3835

Sets	Price
1	$810
5	$860
8	$910
VELLUM	$1095
CD	$1895

REAR ELEVATION

2003 Frank Betz Associates, Inc.

This one-level design is equipped with several added extras that make it original and unique. Just off the kitchen is a vaulted keeping room that is bright and comfortable with radius windows that allow the natural light to illuminate the room. Built-in cabinetry in the family room gives this area an appealing focal point, as well as ample storage and decorating opportunities.

Hennefield

FRANK BETZ ASSOCIATES, INC.

BEDROOMS 4
BATH 3-1/2
WIDTH . . . . 63'0"
DEPTH. . . . . 67'6"
1ST FLOOR. . . . . 2548 sq ft
LIVING AREA . . . . 2548 sq ft
OPT. 2ND FLOOR. . . . . 490 sq ft
FOUNDATION. . . . . . . CRAWL SPACE OR BASEMENT
PLAN NUMBER **SDHFB01-3835**

Floor plan labels

Master Suite 14² x 19⁸
TRAY CEILING
FRENCH DOOR
3'-2" TRANSOMS
FRENCH DOOR
BUILT-IN CABINETS
Breakfast
TRAY CLG.
RADIUS WINDOW
Vaulted Keeping Room 13⁵ x 14⁹
FPL
Vaulted Family Room 16⁵ x 18⁰
FPL
SERVING BAR
REF.
DW.
Kitchen
SURF. UNIT
W.i.c.
Bedroom 2 12⁰ x 11⁰
OVEN/MICRO
ISLAND
PANT.
LINEN
Bath
BUILT-IN CABINETS
FRENCH DOORS
SHWR.
K.S.
Vaulted M.Bath
RADIUS WINDOW
PLANT SHELF ABOVE
LIN.
LINEN
Pwdr.
DECORATIVE COLUMNS
COATS
STAIRS DN.
Bedroom 3 12⁸ x 11⁰
MIRROR
His   Hers
Foyer 12'-0" HIGH CEILING
Dining Room 12⁰ x 13³ 12'-0" HIGH CEILING
Laun.
STAIRS UP
Covered Porch
Garage 22⁷ x 20⁴
COPYRIGHT © 2003 FRANK BETZ ASSOCIATES, INC.

FIRST FLOOR

Optional second floor labels
VAULT
Family Room Below
OPEN RAIL
OVERLOOK
Bonus Room 12⁹ x 16¹⁰
Bedroom 4 11² x 12⁰
Bath
Attic
LINEN
STAIRS DN.

OPT. SECOND FLOOR

© The Sater Design Collection, In

SETS	PRICE
1	N/A
6	$1512
8	N/A
VELLUM	$1512
CD	$2772

REAR VIEW

Jamaican plantation houses inspired this cottage design, lovingly revived by the Old Charleston Row homes. Wraparound porticos on two levels offer views to the living areas, while a deck for stargazing opens from the master suite. French doors bring the outside in to the great room, which features a fireplace, built-ins and an eating bar connecting to the kitchen.

Bridgeport Harbor

THE SATER DESIGN COLLECTION, INC.

BEDROOMS 3
BATH 2-1/2
WIDTH . . . . 30'6"
DEPTH . . . . 77'6"
1ST FLOOR . . . . 1305 sq ft
2ND FLOOR . . . . 1215 sq ft
LIVING AREA . . . . 2520 sq ft
FOUNDATION . . . . SLAB
PLAN NUMBER **SDHDS01-6685**

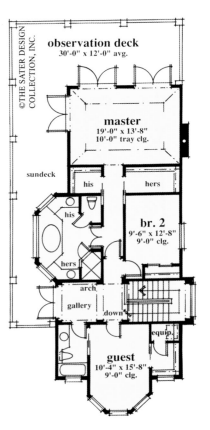

FIRST FLOOR

SECOND FLOOR

LOWER LEVEL

PRICING FOR SDHDG01-540

SETS	PRICE
1	$620
5	$680
8	$730
VELLUM	$1025
CD	$1850

REAR ELEVATION

1997 Donald A. Gardner, Inc.

FIRST FLOOR

- SCREEN PORCH 18-6 x 11-1
- PORCH
- MASTER BED RM. 14-8 x 14-0
- walk-in closet
- skylights
- (cathedral ceiling)
- GREAT RM. 17-4 x 16-6
- BRKFST. 11-0 x 10-2
- skylight
- BED RM. 11-4 x 11-4
- fireplace
- bath
- master bath
- up
- UTIL. 7-8 x 6-0
- storage
- KIT. 9-0 x 12-8
- BED RM. 11-4 x 11-4
- FOYER 5-0 x 11-8
- DINING 13-8 x 11-4
- GARAGE 21-0 x 21-8
- PORCH

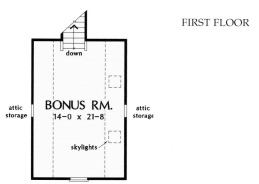

- BONUS RM. 14-0 x 21-8
- down
- attic storage
- attic storage
- skylights

Along with a tray ceiling, columns define the dining room. The great room features a cathedral ceiling and fireplace with built-in. Designed for efficiency, the kitchen opens to the breakfast room and great room and includes a time-saving raised counter for quick meals. The master suite enjoys double-door entry, porch access and a tray ceiling in the bedroom.

Anniston

DONALD A. GARDNER ARCHITECTS, INC.

BEDROOMS	3
BATH	2
WIDTH	64'4"
DEPTH	51'0"
1ST FLOOR	1652 sq ft
LIVING AREA	1652 sq ft
BONUS ROOM	367 sq ft
FOUNDATION	CRAWL SPACE*
PLAN NUMBER	**SDHDG01-540**

*Other options available. See page 175.

PRICING FOR
SDHFB01-3711

SETS	PRICE
1	$685
5	$735
8	$785
VELLUM	$905
CD	$1555

REAR ELEVATION

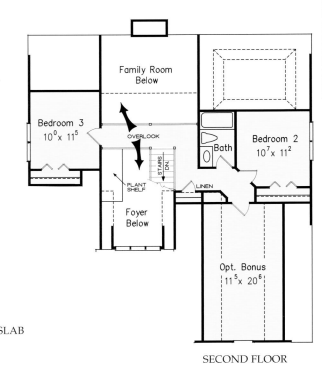

Brick and stone set off by multi-pane windows highlight the street presence of this classic home. A sheltered entry leads to a two-story foyer and wide interior vistas that extend to the back property. Rooms in the public zone are open, allowing the spaces to flex for planned events. At the heart of the home, the vaulted family room frames a fireplace with tall windows that bring in natural light.

Brentwood

FRANK BETZ ASSOCIATES, INC.

BEDROOMS 3
BATH 2-1/2
WIDTH . . . . 41'0"
DEPTH . . . . 48'4"
1ST FLOOR . . . . 1177 sq ft
2ND FLOOR . . . . 457 sq ft
LIVING AREA . . . . 1634 sq ft
OPT. BONUS ROOM . . . 249 sq ft
FOUNDATION . . . . CRAWL SPACE, SLAB OR BASEMENT
PLAN NUMBER **SDHFB01-3711**

© 2002 Frank Betz Associates, Ir

FIRST FLOOR

COPYRIGHT © 2002
FRANK BETZ ASSOCIATES, INC.

SECOND FLOOR

© The Sater Design Collection, Inc.

PRICING FOR SDHDS01-6827

SETS	PRICE
1	N/A
6	$1590
8	N/A
VELLUM	$1590
CD	$2915

REAR ELEVATION

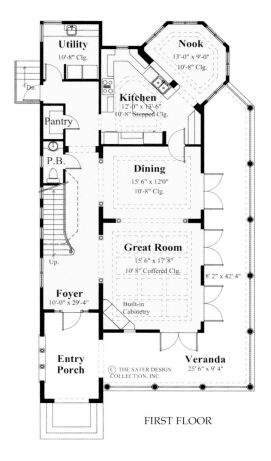

FIRST FLOOR

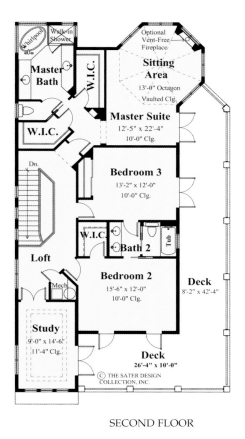

SECOND FLOOR

An elegant portico and deck enhance the outdoor flow of this enchanting manor. All of the living spaces have French doors that open to the porch. A gallery-style foyer leads to a powder room and a walk-in pantry, which enhances the efficiency of the kitchen. Wrapping counter space provides an overlook to a breakfast bay boasting 180-degree views of the rear.

Sommerset

THE SATER DESIGN COLLECTION, INC.

BEDROOMS 3
BATH 2-1/2
WIDTH . . . . 34'0"
DEPTH . . . . 63'2"
1ST FLOOR . . . . 1296 sq ft
2ND FLOOR . . . . 1354 sq ft
LIVING AREA . . . . 2650 sq ft
FOUNDATION . . . . SLAB
PLAN NUMBER **SDHDS01-6827**

© 2003 Donald A. Gardner, Inc

PRICING FOR SDHDG01-1036

Sets	Price
1	$620
5	$680
8	$730
VELLUM	$1025
CD	$1850

REAR ELEVATION

Gables and columns set the stage for a low-maintenance Traditional that's big on living. Open common rooms separate the master suite from secondary bedrooms. A tray ceiling and column highlight the dining room, and a cathedral ceiling crowns the great room. Porches provide outdoor living space, and a bonus room offers versatility. Windows keep the breakfast nook bright and airy.

Pinebluff

DONALD A. GARDNER ARCHITECTS, INC.

BEDROOMS 3
BATH 2
WIDTH . . . . 52'11"
DEPTH . . . . 54'2"
1ST FLOOR . . . . 1614 sq ft
LIVING AREA . . . . 1614 sq ft
BONUS ROOM . . . . 410 sq ft
FOUNDATION . . . . CRAWL SPACE*
PLAN NUMBER **SDHDG01-1036**

*Other options available. See page 175.

BONUS RM.
15-0 x 22-0

attic storage   down   attic storage

MASTER BED RM.
12-8 x 14-0
(cathedral ceiling)

BRKFST.
9-8 x 8-4

PORCH

cl   walk-in closet

KIT.
9-8 x 9-0

up

master bath

d   w   **UTIL.**
9-8 x 6-0

fireplace

GREAT RM.
16-8 x 16-4
(cathedral ceiling)

BED RM.
11-4 x 12-4

cl

lin.

bath

cl

(optional door)

DINING
11-0 x 12-0

FOYER
5-4 x 12-0

BED RM./STUDY
11-4 x 12-4
(cathedral ceiling)

GARAGE
22-8 x 22-0

PORCH

© 2003 DONALD A. GARDNER
All rights reserved

FIRST FLOOR

© The Sater Design Collection, Inc.

PRICING FOR
SDHDS01-6858

SETS	PRICE
1	N/A
6	$1654
8	N/A
VELLUM	$1654
CD	$3032

REAR ELEVATION

LOWER LEVEL

FIRST FLOOR

SECOND FLOOR

This Southern tidewater cottage is charming with a horizontal siding exterior and inviting wraparound front-entry porch. An octagonal great room with a multi-faceted vaulted ceiling illuminates the interior. This room boasts a fireplace, a built-in entertainment center and three sets of French doors, which lead outside to a vaulted lanai.

Montserrat

THE SATER DESIGN COLLECTION, INC.

BEDROOMS 3
BATH 3-1/2
WIDTH . . . . 66'0"
DEPTH. . . . . 50'0"
1ST FLOOR. . . . . 1855 sq ft
2ND FLOOR. . . . . 901 sq ft
LIVING AREA . . . . 2756 sq ft
FOUNDATION. . . . . . . ISLAND BASMENT
PLAN NUMBER **SDHDS01-6858**

PRICING FOR
SDHFB01-992

SETS	PRICE
1	$870
5	$920
8	$970
VELLUM	$1190
CD	$2065

REAR ELEVATION

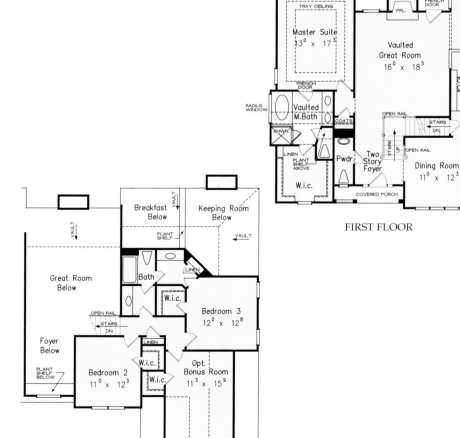

Everyone knows that family members and guests tend to congregate in the kitchen. The *Mallory* accommodates this fact, with a vaulted breakfast area and keeping room with fireplace adjoining the kitchen. Two secondary bedrooms — each with a walk-in closet — share a divided bathing area on the second floor. An optional bonus room is ready to finish into a fourth bedroom, playroom or exercise area.

Mallory

FRANK BETZ ASSOCIATES, INC.

BEDROOMS 3
BATH 2-1/2
WIDTH . . . . 54'0"
DEPTH . . . . 46'10"
1ST FLOOR . . . . 1628 sq ft
2ND FLOOR . . . . 527 sq ft
LIVING AREA . . . . 2155 sq ft
OPT. BONUS ROOM . . . 207 sq ft
FOUNDATION . . . . CRAWL SPACE, SLAB OR BASEMENT
PLAN NUMBER **SDHFB01-992**

© 1996 Frank Betz Associates, Inc.

SECOND FLOOR

FIRST FLOOR

COPYRIGHT © 1996
FRANK BETZ ASSOCIATES, INC.

REAR ELEVATION

2006 Visbeen Associates, Inc.

FRONT ELEVATION

PRICING FOR SDHVA01-9032

SETS	PRICE
VELLUM	$2095
PRINTABLE PDF ON DISK	$1795

FIRST FLOOR

Bath

Kit.
14'-0" x 11'-9"

Pantry

Liv.
15'-0" x 23'-4"

Bdrm.
11'-10" x 10'-2"

Din.
14'-0" x 11'-1"

UP

SECOND FLOOR

Bdrm.
12'-4" x 21'-4"

DOWN

Bdrm.
9'-10" x 21'-4"

Bath

Less truly is more in this custom-designed home which recalls the simple bungalows and cottages of the past yet is designed for the way people live today. A shingle and stone exterior leads to an open floor plan, where an adjacent living, dining and kitchen area makes up the heart of the home. The first floor also includes a spacious master suite, while two additional bedrooms upstairs allows for much-needed privacy.

Dune View

VISBEEN ASSOCIATES, INC.

BEDROOMS 3
BATH 2
WIDTH . . . . 46'0"
DEPTH . . . . 26'5"
1ST FLOOR . . . . 1005 sq ft
2ND FLOOR . . . . 687 sq ft
LIVING AREA . . . . 1692 sq ft
FOUNDATION . . . . CRAWL SPACE
PLAN NUMBER SDHVA01-9032

PRICING FOR SDHDS01-6845

SETS	PRICE
1	N/A
6	$1410
8	N/A
VELLUM	$1410
CD	$2585

REAR VIEW

This enticing European villa boasts an Italian charm and a distinctly Mediterranean feel. Inside, the foyer steps lead up to the formal living areas. Vaulted ceilings create a sense of spaciousness throughout the home, and enhance the interior vistas provided by the central great room, which overlooks the rear deck. The island kitchen is conveniently open to a breakfast nook.

Mission Hills

THE SATER DESIGN COLLECTION, INC.

BEDROOMS 3
BATH 3
WIDTH . . . . 60'0"
DEPTH. . . . . 60'0"
1ST FLOOR. . . . . 2350 sq ft
LIVING AREA . . . . 2350 sq ft
FOUNDATION. . . . . . . ISLAND BASEMENT
PLAN NUMBER. **SDHDS01-6845**

©THE SATER DESIGN COLLECTION, INC.

FIRST FLOOR

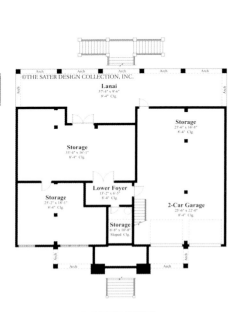

LOWER LEVEL

PRICING FOR SDHDS01-6692	
SETS	PRICE
1	N/A
6	$1314
8	N/A
VELLUM	$1314
CD	$2409

REAR ELEVATION

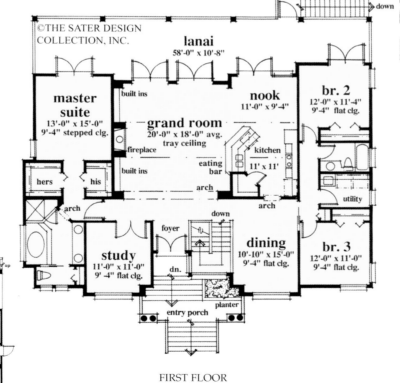

©THE SATER DESIGN COLLECTION, INC.

lanai
58'-0" x 10'-8"

master suite
13'-0" x 15'-0"
9'-4" stepped clg.

built ins

nook
11'-0" x 9'-4"

br. 2
12'-0" x 11'-4"
9'-4" flat clg.

grand room
20'-0" x 18'-0" avg.
tray ceiling

fireplace

kitchen
11' x 11'

hers   his

built ins

eating bar

arch

arch

utility

foyer

down

study
11'-0" x 11'-0"
9'-4" flat clg.

dn.

dining
10'-10" x 15'-0"
9'-4" flat clg.

br. 3
12'-0" x 11'-0"
9'-4" flat clg.

arch

entry porch

planter

FIRST FLOOR

verandah
58'-0" x 12'-0"

recreation
25'-0" x 35'-0"

storage

garage
23'-4" x 24'-0"

©THE SATER DESIGN COLLECTION, INC.

LOWER LEVEL

The arched entry of this Southampton-style cottage borrows freely from its Southern coastal past. The foyer opens up to the spacious grand room, which features a fireplace, built-ins and French doors to the lanai. A well-crafted kitchen boasts wrapping counter space, a casual eating bar, a corner walk-in pantry and easy access to the formal dining room.

Tuckertown Way

THE SATER DESIGN COLLECTION, INC.

BEDROOMS 3
BATH 2
WIDTH . . . . 59'8"
DEPTH. . . . . 54'0"
1ST FLOOR. . . . . 2190 sq ft
LIVING AREA . . . . 2190 sq ft
FOUNDATION. . . . . ISLAND BASEMENT
PLAN NUMBER. **SDHDS01-6692**

PRICING FOR
SDHDG01-782

Sets	Price
1	$620
5	$680
8	$730
VELLUM	$1025
CD	$1850

REAR ELEVATION

A trio of dormers with arch-topped windows and a country porch adorn the façade of this gracious home. Columns and a tray ceiling grant distinction and definition to the formal dining room, while the great room is enriched by a cathedral ceiling with two rear clerestory dormers, a fireplace and built-in bookshelves.

Riverbirch

DONALD A. GARDNER ARCHITECTS, INC.

BEDROOMS 3
BATH 2
WIDTH . . . . 65'8"
DEPTH . . . . 49'8"
1ST FLOOR . . . . 1733 sq ft
LIVING AREA . . . . 1733 sq ft
BONUS ROOM . . . . 372 sq ft
FOUNDATION . . . . CRAWL SPACE*
PLAN NUMBER **SDHDG01-782**

*Other options available. See page 175.

FIRST FLOOR

PORCH

BED RM.
11-0 x 13-8

GREAT RM.
20-0 x 16-0
(cathedral ceiling)

BRKFST.
10-0 x 9-0

KIT.
12-0 x
11-0

MASTER
BED RM.
13-4 x 16-0

lin.

master
bath

walk-in
closet

storage

cl

lin.

bath

BED RM./
STUDY
11-0 x 11-0

FOYER
6-4 x
11-0

DINING
13-4 x 11-0

UTIL.
6-0 x
7-0

up

GARAGE
21-0 x 21-0

cl

cl

PORCH

BONUS RM.
13-4 x 21-0

down

attic
storage

attic
storage

PRICING FOR SDHFB01-3896

SETS	PRICE
1	$810
5	$860
8	$910
VELLUM	$1095
CD	$1895

© 2004 Frank Betz Associates, Inc.

REAR ELEVATION

FIRST FLOOR

Screened Porch
14⁶ x 11⁸

TRAY CEILING

Master Suite
13² x 17⁰

Family Room
16⁰ x 19⁰
12'-6" HIGH
COFFERED CEILING

FRENCH DOOR

2'-0" TRANSOMS

BUILT-IN CABINETS

Breakfast

W.i.c.

PANT.

Bedroom 2
12⁰ x 11⁰

SERVING BAR

Kitchen

REF.

Bath

TRAY CLG.

M.Bath

Pwdr.

Foyer

Dining Room
12⁰ x 14²

Mudroom

Bedroom 3
12⁰ x 12⁰

BENCH

SHWR.

LINEN

W.i.c.

COVERED ENTRY

COVERED ENTRY

COATS

Laund.

W.i.c.

Garage
20⁵ x 24⁵

COPYRIGHT © 2004
FRANK BETZ ASSOCIATES, INC.

OPT. SECOND FLOOR

Bedroom 4
15³ x 13³

W.i.c.

Bath

LINEN

OPEN RAIL STAIRS

DN.

Bonus Room
12⁰ x 12²

Attic

The *Colemans Bluff* is original and inviting with a coffered ceiling providing a unique canopy over the family room. A large screened porch off the breakfast area provides the perfect spot for outdoor living. The garage entry filters traffic through the mudroom, fully equipped with a coat closet, bench, wall hooks and access to the laundry room.

Colemans Bluff

FRANK BETZ ASSOCIATES, INC.

BEDROOMS 4
BATH 3-1/2
WIDTH . . . . 63'0"
DEPTH . . . . 79'4"
1ST FLOOR . . . . 2066 sq ft
LIVING AREA . . . . 2066 sq ft
OPT. 2ND FLOOR . . . . . 556 sq ft
FOUNDATION . . . . CRAWL SPACE, SLAB OR BASEMENT
PLAN NUMBER **SDHFB01-3896**

PRICING FOR SDHDS01-6807

SETS	PRICE
1	N/A
6	$1187
8	N/A
VELLUM	$1187
CD	$2176

REAR ELEVATION

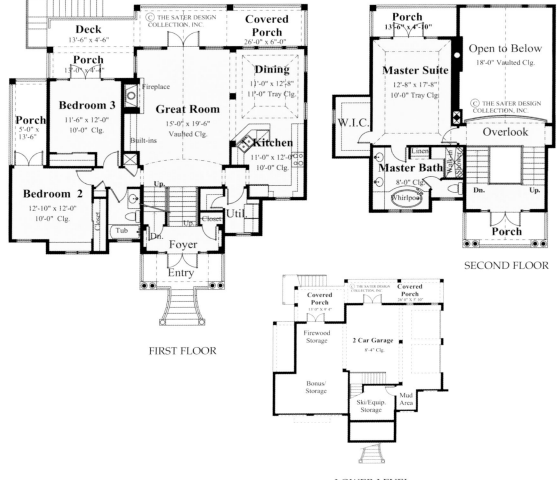

Asymmetrical gables and decorative shutters combine with a bold mix of textures to create a refined rustic feel. Inside, the open floor plan encourages flow between the common living areas and the back porch. Built-ins, a fireplace, vaulted ceilings and extensive views through a wall of windows add to the appeal of the great room. Wrapping counters, an angled double sink and ample storage enhance the kitchen.

Buckhurst Lodge

THE SATER DESIGN COLLECTION, INC.

BEDROOMS 3
BATH 2
WIDTH . . . . 48'0"
DEPTH . . . . 42'0"
1ST FLOOR . . . . 1383 sq ft
2ND FLOOR . . . . 595 sq ft
LIVING AREA . . . . 1978 sq ft
FOUNDATION . . . . ISLAND BASEMENT
PLAN NUMBER **SDHDS01-6807**

FIRST FLOOR

SECOND FLOOR

LOWER LEVEL

**PRICING FOR
SDHDG01-839**

SETS	PRICE
1	$575
5	$630
8	$685
VELLUM	$960
CD	$1720

REAR ELEVATION

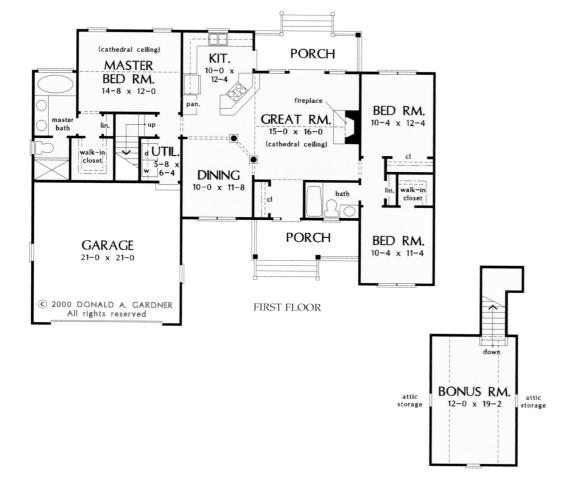

(cathedral ceiling)

**MASTER
BED RM.**
14-8 x 12-0

master
bath

lin.

walk-in
closet

up

KIT.
10-0 x
12-4

pan.

PORCH

fireplace

GREAT RM.
15-0 x 16-0
(cathedral ceiling)

BED RM.
10-4 x 12-4

UTIL.
5-8 x
6-4

DINING
10-0 x 11-8

cl

bath

cl

lin.

walk-in
closet

GARAGE
21-0 x 21-0

PORCH

BED RM.
10-4 x 11-4

FIRST FLOOR

down

attic
storage

BONUS RM.
12-0 x 19-2

attic
storage

This modest home makes the most of its square footage by utilizing a very open floor plan and volume ceilings to create a feeling of spaciousness. A split bedroom design gives the master suite privacy from two secondary bedrooms. A cathedral ceiling expands the master bedroom, which features a linen closet, walk-in closet, and bath with garden tub and shower.

Blakely

DONALD A. GARDNER ARCHITECTS, INC.

BEDROOMS	3
BATH	2
WIDTH	58'0"
DEPTH	44'4"
1ST FLOOR	1399 sq ft
LIVING AREA	1399 sq ft
BONUS ROOM	296 sq ft
FOUNDATION	CRAWL SPACE*
PLAN NUMBER	**SDHDG01-839**

*Other options available. See page 175.

PRICING FOR
SDHDG01-979

SETS	PRICE
1	$620
5	$680
8	$730
VELLUM	$1025
CD	$1850

REAR ELEVATION

Incorporating Old-World style, stone and shake with gables and arched windows creates a stunning façade. The portico leads to an open floor plan. Built-ins, French doors and a fireplace enhance the great room, while a counter separates the kitchen from the breakfast nook. The master suite is located in the quiet zone, and a balcony overlooks the great room.

Luxembourg

DONALD A. GARDNER ARCHITECTS, INC.

BEDROOMS 3
BATH 2-1/2
WIDTH . . . . 63'0"
DEPTH . . . . 40'0"
1ST FLOOR . . . . 1345 sq ft
2ND FLOOR . . . . 452 sq ft
LIVING AREA . . . . 1797 sq ft
BONUS ROOM . . . . 349 sq ft
FOUNDATION . . . . CRAWL SPACE*
PLAN NUMBER **SDHDG01-979**

*Other options available. See page 175.

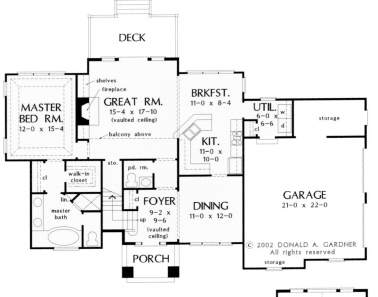

FIRST FLOOR

SECOND FLOOR

Compact Luxury

PRICING FOR SDHDS01-8058

SETS	PRICE
1	N/A
6	$1900
8	N/A
VELLUM	$1900
CD	$3483

REAR ELEVATION

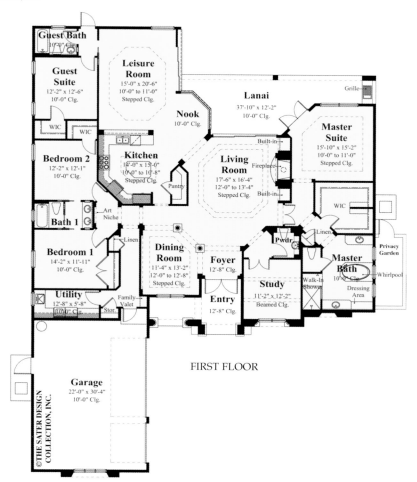

FIRST FLOOR

Guest Bath
10'-0" Clg.

Guest Suite
12'-2" x 12'-6"
10'-0" Clg.

WIC WIC

Bedroom 2
12'-2" x 12'-1"
10'-0" Clg.

Kitchen
14'-0" x 15'-0"
10'-0" to 10'-8"
Stepped Clg.

Pantry

Bath 1

Art Niche

Linen

Bedroom 1
14'-2" x 11'-11"
10'-0" Clg.

Utility
12'-8" x 5'-8"
10'-0" Clg.

Family Valet

Stor.

Dining Room
11'-4" x 13'-2"
12'-0" to 12'-8"
Stepped Clg.

Leisure Room
15'-0" x 20'-6"
10'-0" to 11'-0"
Stepped Clg.

Nook
10'-0" Clg.

Lanai
37'-10" x 12'-2"
10'-0" Clg.

Grille

Living Room
17'-6" x 16'-4"
12'-0" to 13'-4"
Stepped Clg.

Built-in

Fireplace

Built-in

Master Suite
15'-10" x 15'-2"
10'-0" to 11'-0"
Stepped Clg.

WIC

Linen

Foyer
12'-8" Clg.

Entry
12'-8" Clg.

Pwdr.

Study
11'-2" x 12'-2"
Beamed Clg.

Master Bath
10'-0" Clg.

Walk-In Shower

Dressing Area

Whirlpool

Privacy Garden

Garage
22'-0" x 30'-4"
10'-0" Clg.

Decorative tile vents, spiral pilasters and wrought-iron window treatments achieve a seamless fusion with the new-century look of this modern revival elevation. Fresh breezes flow through the plan, with walls of glass that extend living spaces to the outdoors. A high-beamed ceiling, crafted cabinetry and a massive hearth achieve a colonial character that is seamlessly fused with state-of-the-art amenities: retreating walls, wide-open rooms, and sleek, do-everything appliances.

Porta Rossa

THE SATER DESIGN COLLECTION, INC.

BEDROOMS 4
BATH 3-1/2
WIDTH . . . . 67'0"
DEPTH . . . . 91'8"
1ST FLOOR . . . . 3166 sq ft
LIVING AREA . . . . 3166 sq ft
FOUNDATION . . . . SLAB
PLAN NUMBER **SDHDS01-8058**

PRICING FOR
SDHFB01-3764

SETS	PRICE
1	$870
5	$920
8	$970
VELLUM	$1190
CD	$2065

REAR ELEVATION

Thoughtful and creative design makes the *Greythorne* unique in both the layout and the details. The full-service kitchen has an attention-grabbing coffered ceiling. Adjoining this room is a vaulted keeping room with a fireplace. Accessible from both the master suite and the keeping room is a covered back porch.

Greythorne

FRANK BETZ ASSOCIATES, INC.

BEDROOMS 4
BATH 3
WIDTH . . . . 60'0"
DEPTH . . . . 56'0"
1ST FLOOR . . . . 2047 sq ft
2ND FLOOR . . . . 540 sq ft
LIVING AREA . . . . 2587 sq ft
OPT. BONUS ROOM . . . 278 sq ft
FOUNDATION . . . . CRAWL SPACE, SLAB
OR BASEMENT
PLAN NUMBER **SDHFB01-3764**

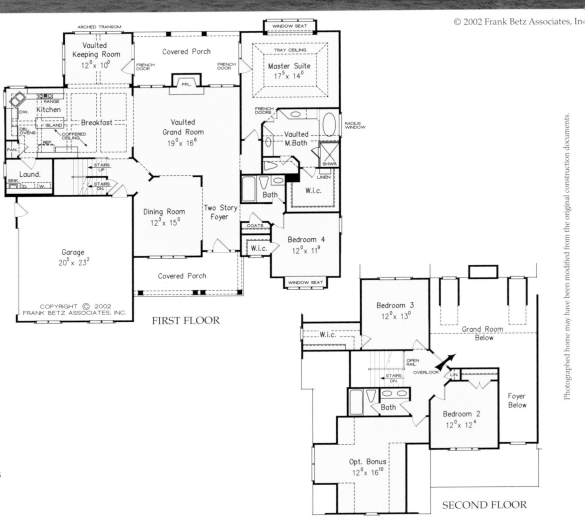

FIRST FLOOR

SECOND FLOOR

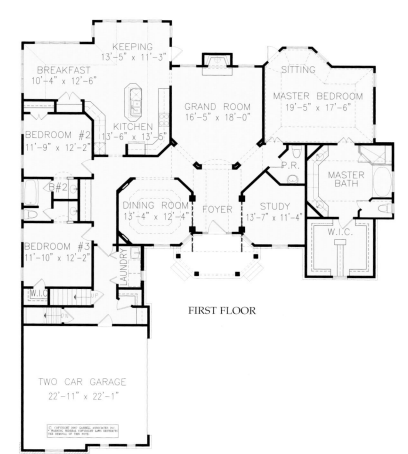

PRICING FOR
SDHGA01-99056

SETS	PRICE
1	N/A
5	$1195
8	N/A
VELLUM	$1295
CD	$2145

REAR ELEVATION

A beautiful covered porch of columns and arches welcomes you into this exciting ranch-style home. A well-designed, split-bedroom plan provides privacy for all. Natural light fills the kitchen, breakfast and keeping room area. Ample storage or a special option is a fourth bedroom suite above the garage.

Weston

GARRELL ASSOCIATES, INC.

BEDROOMS 3
BATH 2-1/2
WIDTH . . . . 66'0"
DEPTH. . . . . 79'8"
1ST FLOOR. . . . . 2663 sq ft
LIVING AREA . . . . 2663 sq ft
OPT. BEDROOM . . . . . . 324 sq ft
FOUNDATION. . . . . SLAB OR BASEMENT
PLAN NUMBER. **SDHGA01-99056**

FIRST FLOOR

KEEPING 13'-5" x 11'-3"
BREAKFAST 10'-4" x 12'-6"
SITTING
GRAND ROOM 16'-5" x 18'-0"
MASTER BEDROOM 19'-5" x 17'-6"
BEDROOM #2 11'-9" x 12'-2"
KITCHEN 13'-6" x 13'-5"
B#2
P.R.
MASTER BATH
DINING ROOM 13'-4" x 12'-4"
FOYER
STUDY 13'-7" x 11'-4"
W.I.C.
BEDROOM #3 11'-10" x 12'-2"
LAUNDRY
W.I.C.
TWO CAR GARAGE 22'-11" x 22'-1"

OPT. BEDROOM

W.I.C.
B#3
STORAGE / OPT. BEDROOM #4 11'-9" x 25'-5"

© The Sater Design Collection, Inc

REAR ELEVATION

Triple arches—in the entryway and windows to the right of the home—create a commanding street presence. Inside, stepped ceilings define the formal rooms with retreating glass walls extending the space outside to the lanai. Down the hall, the kitchen/nook/leisure room area acts as the natural hub of the home, with guest bedrooms conveniently nearby. Away from the public rooms, the master retreat enjoys quiet seclusion in the opposite wing of the home.

Royal Palm

THE SATER DESIGN COLLECTION, INC.

BEDROOMS 3
BATH 2-1/2
WIDTH .... 65'0"
DEPTH .... 85'4"
1ST FLOOR .... 2823 sq ft
LIVING AREA .... 2823 sq ft
FOUNDATION .... SLAB
PLAN NUMBER **SDHDS01-6727**

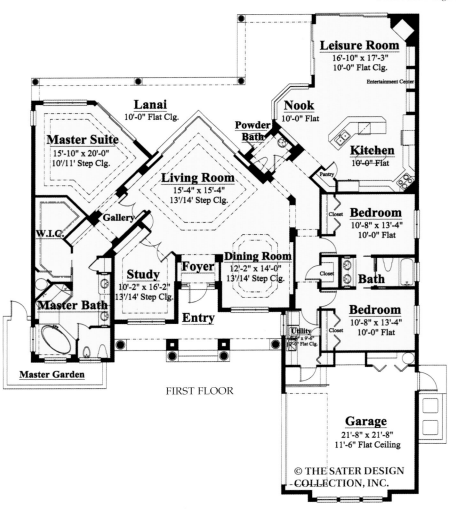

FIRST FLOOR

© THE SATER DESIGN COLLECTION, INC.

© 2003 Visbeen Associates, Inc.

PRICING FOR SDHVA01-9015

SETS	PRICE
VELLUM	$2595
PRINTABLE PDF ON DISK	$2295

REAR ELEVATION

SCREEN PORCH

Bdrm.
14'-8" x 15'-0"

Mbr.
14'-8" x 15'-2"

Bath

Bath

WIC

Bdrm.
13'-0" x 13'-0"

© VISBEEN ASSOCIATES, Inc.

Recreation Room

SECOND FLOOR

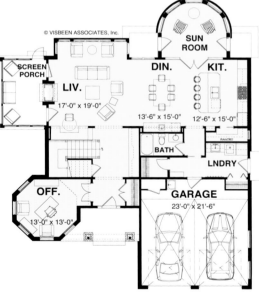

© VISBEEN ASSOCIATES, Inc.

SCREEN PORCH

LIV.
17'-0" x 19'-0"

DIN.
13'-6" x 15'-0"

SUN ROOM

KIT.
12'-6" x 15'-0"

BATH

LNDRY

OFF.
13'-0" x 13'-0"

GARAGE
23'-0" x 21'-6"

FIRST FLOOR

Family Room
26'-5" x 20'-0"

Bdrm.
16'-6" x 14'-2"

© Visbeen Associates, Inc.

OPT. THIRD FLOOR

The best of American and European traditions merge in this sunny and spacious floor plan. Featured are a formal living room with large fireplace, an octagonal home office, a kitchen complete with eating bar, adjacent sun room and more. The spacious master suite includes a generous walk-in closet and private screen porch. Nearby are three additional upstairs bedrooms, while the lower level features an additional bedroom and a welcoming family room.

Wyndham

VISBEEN ASSOCIATES, INC.

BEDROOMS	4
BATH	4
WIDTH	54'0"
DEPTH	65'0"
1ST FLOOR	1714 sq ft
2ND FLOOR	1461 sq ft
OPT. 3RD FLOOR	1030 sq ft
LIVING AREA	3175 sq ft
FOUNDATION	CRAWL SPACE
PLAN NUMBER	SDHVA01-9015

Compact Luxury

REAR ELEVATION

Compact yet charming, this home includes all the details of a much larger home. The European exterior features a stone entrance and copper roofing over the bedroom/study window. The great room and stunning dining room are crowned with tray ceilings, lending formal drama. The secondary bedrooms are positioned for privacy.

Runnymeade

DONALD A. GARDNER ARCHITECTS, INC.

BEDROOMS 3
BATH 2
WIDTH . . . . 60'0"
DEPTH . . . . 51'5"
1ST FLOOR . . . . 1583 sq ft
LIVING AREA . . . . 1583 sq ft
BONUS ROOM . . . . 403 sq ft
FOUNDATION . . . . CRAWL SPACE*
PLAN NUMBER **SDHDG01-1164**

*Other options available. See page 175.

FIRST FLOOR

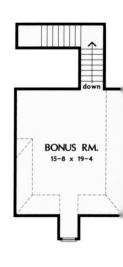

PRICING FOR SDHDS01-8004

SETS	PRICE
1	N/A
6	$1982
8	N/A
VELLUM	$1982
CD	$3634

REAR ELEVATION

The Sater Design Collection, Inc.

FIRST FLOOR

SECOND FLOOR

Stacked stone and stucco capture the character of a rural Italian manor. Inside, an open foyer is defined by columns and arches, allowing views that extend past the veranda. Architectural details—a coffered ceiling above the two-story great room, an art niche and built-in cabinetry—contribute to the rustic décor. State-of-the-art appliances in the kitchen and computer loft play counterpoint to rough-hewn ceiling beams and stone accents in the nook and study.

Chadbryne

THE SATER DESIGN COLLECTION, INC.

BEDROOMS 4
BATH 3-1/2
WIDTH . . . . 91'0"
DEPTH. . . . . 52'8"
1ST FLOOR. . . . . 2219 sq ft
2ND FLOOR. . . . . 1085 sq ft
LIVING AREA . . . . 3304 sq ft
BONUS ROOM. . . . . . . 404 sq ft
FOUNDATION. . . . . SLAB OR
OPT. BASEMENT
PLAN NUMBER **SDHDS01-8004**

PRICING FOR
SDHDS01-6784

SETS	PRICE
1	N/A
6	$1910
8	N/A
VELLUM	$1910
CD	$3502

© The Sater Design Collection, In

REAR ELEVATION

Arches, columns and a corner courtyard adorn this charming villa. Inside, a smart floor plan loaded with glass walls and windows enhances indoor-outdoor living. Past the foyer, the formal living and dining rooms are divided by a floating bar and bordered by pocketing glass walls to the lanai. A butler's pantry connects the formal rooms to the kitchen, ensuring easy entertaining.

Rosario

THE SATER DESIGN COLLECTION, INC.

BEDROOMS 3
BATH 3-1/2
WIDTH . . . . 65'0"
DEPTH . . . . 90'6"
1ST FLOOR . . . . 3184 sq ft
LIVING AREA . . . . 3184 sq ft
FOUNDATION . . . . SLAB
PLAN NUMBER **SDHDS01-6784**

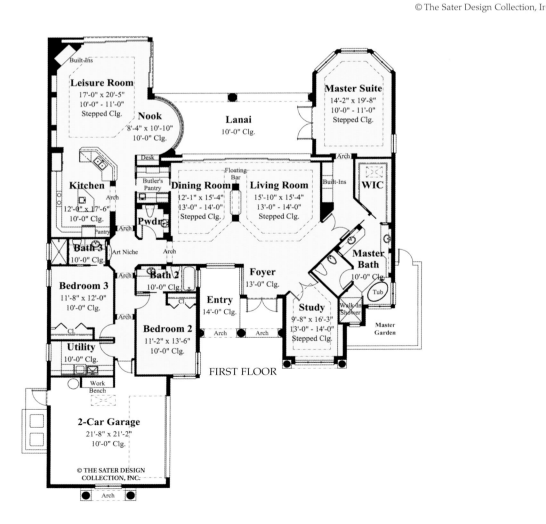

Compact Luxury

PRICING FOR SDHFB01-3946

SETS	PRICE
1	$810
5	$860
8	$910
VELLUM	$1095
CD	$1895

REAR ELEVATION

The European look of the *Heritage Pointe* would be ideal for a mountain community. A teen loft on the second floor has a window seat and the option to include a closet. The master suite occupies one wing of the home and features a vaulted ceiling. The vaulted family room has built-in bookshelves, a fireplace and views to rear of the home.

Heritage Pointe

FRANK BETZ ASSOCIATES, INC.

BEDROOMS 5
BATH 3
WIDTH . . . . 59'0"
DEPTH . . . . 52'0"
1ST FLOOR . . . . 1959 sq ft
2ND FLOOR . . . . 817 sq ft
LIVING AREA . . . . 2776 sq ft
OPT. BONUS ROOM . . . 271 sq ft
FOUNDATION . . . . CRAWL SPACE
OR BASEMENT
PLAN NUMBER **SDHFB01-3946**

SECOND FLOOR

FIRST FLOOR

PRICING FOR
SDHDS01-6602

SETS	PRICE
1	N/A
6	$1676
8	N/A
VELLUM	$1676
CD	$3073

REAR VIEW

© The Sater Design Collection, In

Decorative columns, circle-head windows and a double-arched entryway add curb appeal to this view-oriented design. Inside the foyer, a mitered glass window provides open views. The formal living and dining rooms are straight ahead, with a unique buffet server connecting the rooms. Blending with the outdoors, nearly every room to the rear of the plan opens to the verandah.

Turnberry Lane

THE SATER DESIGN COLLECTION, INC.

BEDROOMS 3
BATH 3
WIDTH . . . . 70'0"
DEPTH . . . . 98'0"
1ST FLOOR . . . . 2794 sq ft
LIVING AREA . . . . 2794 sq ft
FOUNDATION . . . . SLAB
PLAN NUMBER **SDHDS01-6602**

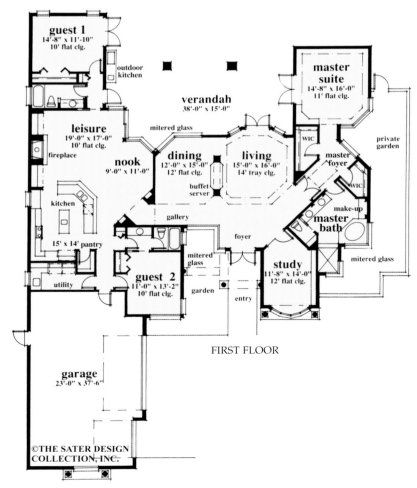

FIRST FLOOR

©THE SATER DESIGN COLLECTION, INC.

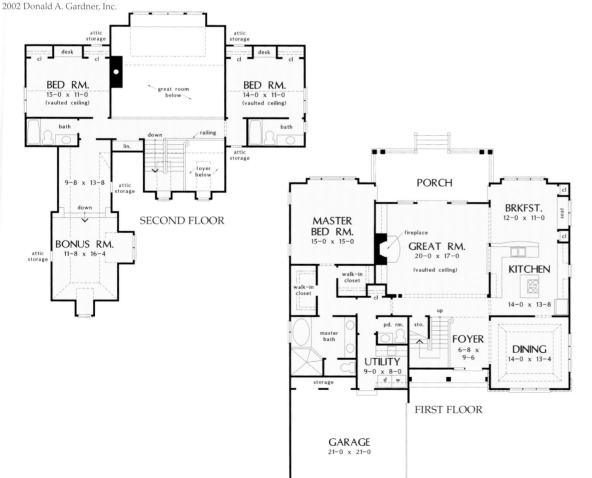

PRICING FOR SDHDG01-994

SETS	PRICE
1	$710
5	$770
8	$820
VELLUM	$1155
CD	$2110

REAR ELEVATION

SECOND FLOOR

attic storage

desk · cl · cl · desk

BED RM.
15–0 x 11–0
(vaulted ceiling)

great room below

BED RM.
14–0 x 11–0
(vaulted ceiling)

bath · bath

down · railing · attic storage

lin.

foyer below

attic storage

9–8 x 13–8

down

attic storage

BONUS RM.
11–8 x 16–4

attic storage

FIRST FLOOR

PORCH

MASTER BED RM.
15–0 x 15–0

fireplace

GREAT RM.
20–0 x 17–0
(vaulted ceiling)

walk-in closet

walk-in closet

cl

BRKFST.
12–0 x 11–0

seat · cl · cl

KITCHEN
14–0 x 13–8

master bath

pd. rm. · sto.

up

UTILITY
9–0 x 8–0

d · w

FOYER
6–8 x 9–6

DINING
14–0 x 13–4

storage

GARAGE
21–0 x 21–0

With Old-World charm on the exterior, the modern gathering rooms are open to each other, distinguished by columns and ceiling treatments. The foyer and great room have two-story ceilings – brightened by dormers, and the fireplace is flanked by built-ins. The breakfast nook includes two pantries, and the kitchen features a cooktop island. Upstairs, a balcony separates two additional bedrooms.

Newcastle

DONALD A. GARDNER ARCHITECTS, INC.

BEDROOMS 3
BATH 3-1/2
WIDTH . . . . 50'8"
DEPTH . . . . 66'8"
1ST FLOOR . . . . 1834 sq ft
2ND FLOOR . . . . 681 sq ft
LIVING AREA . . . . 2515 sq ft
BONUS ROOM . . . . 365 sq ft
FOUNDATION . . . . CRAWL SPACE*
PLAN NUMBER **SDHDG01-994**

*Other options available. See page 175.

SETS	PRICE
1	$810
5	$860
8	$910
VELLUM	$1095
CD	$1895

REAR ELEVATION

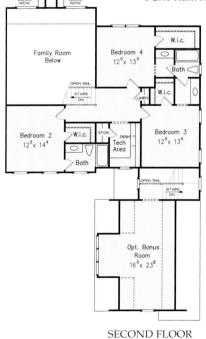

The beamed tray ceiling of the master suite makes the *Keene's Point* perfect for a mountain or lake home. A rear deck off the kitchen makes entertaining fun and convenient. A suite on the main level offers guests access to a private bath and a walk-in closet. Three bedrooms and an optional bonus room complete the second floor.

Keenes Pointe

FRANK BETZ ASSOCIATES, INC.

BEDROOMS 5
BATH 4
WIDTH . . . . 54'0"
DEPTH . . . . 70'4"
1ST FLOOR . . . . 1895 sq ft
2ND FLOOR . . . . 963 sq ft
LIVING AREA . . . . 2858 sq ft
OPT. BONUS ROOM . . . 352 sq ft
FOUNDATION . . . . CRAWL SPACE
OR BASEMENT
PLAN NUMBER **SDHFB01-3940**

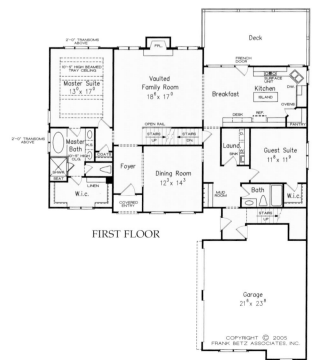

© 2005 Frank Betz Associates, Inc

SECOND FLOOR

FIRST FLOOR

COPYRIGHT © 2005
FRANK BETZ ASSOCIATES, INC.

The Sater Design Collection, Inc.

PRICING FOR SDHDS01-6778

SETS	PRICE
1	N/A
6	$1745
8	N/A
VELLUM	$1745
CD	$3199

REAR VIEW

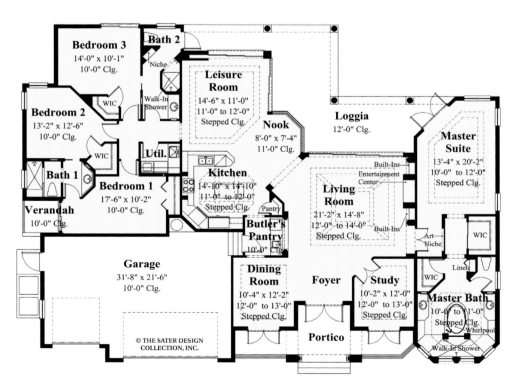

FIRST FLOOR

Bedroom 3
14'-0" x 10'-1"
10'-0" Clg.

Bath 2

Niche

WIC

Walk-In Shower

Bedroom 2
13'-2" x 12'-6"
10'-0" Clg.

WIC

Util.

Bath 1

Bedroom 1
17'-6" x 10'-2"
10'-0" Clg.

Verandah
10'-0" Clg.

Leisure Room
14'-6" x 11'-0"
11'-0" to 12'-0"
Stepped Clg.

Nook
8'-0" x 7'-4"
11'-0" Clg.

Kitchen
14'-10" x 14'-10"
11'-0" to 12'-0"
Stepped Clg.

Pantry

Butler's Pantry
10'-0" Clg.

Loggia
12'-0" Clg.

Master Suite
13'-4" x 20'-2"
10'-0" to 12'-0"
Stepped Clg.

Built-Ins

Entertainment Center

Living Room
21'-2" x 14'-8"
12'-0" to 14'-0"
Stepped Clg.

Built-Ins

Art Niche

WIC

Linen

WIC

Garage
31'-8" x 21'-6"
10'-0" Clg.

© THE SATER DESIGN COLLECTION, INC.

Dining Room
10'-4" x 12'-2"
12'-0" to 13'-0"
Stepped Clg.

Foyer

Study
10'-2" x 12'-0"
12'-0" to 13'-0"
Stepped Clg.

Master Bath
10'-0" to 11'-0"
Stepped Clg.
Whirlpool

Walk-In Shower

Portico

Repeating arches line the portico entry of this Italianate-style home. Just past the foyer, the living room features a built-in entertainment center and retreating glass walls to the loggia. A butler's pantry connects the formal dining room to the gourmet-caliber kitchen. Nearby, a family-friendly leisure room opens to the loggia, making indoor/outdoor entertaining easy. Away from the public realms, the master retreat enjoys the entire right wing of the home.

Deauville

THE SATER DESIGN COLLECTION, INC.

BEDROOMS 4
BATH 3
WIDTH . . . . 80'10"
DEPTH . . . . 59'10"
1ST FLOOR . . . . 2908 sq ft
LIVING AREA . . . . 2908 sq ft
FOUNDATION . . . . SLAB
PLAN NUMBER **SDHDS01-6778**

PRICING FOR
SDHGA01-06073

SETS	PRICE
1	N/A
5	$1538
8	N/A
VELLUM	$1638
CD	$2488

© 2000-2007 Garrell Associates, In

REAR ELEVATION

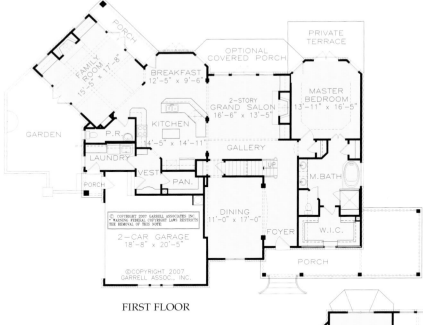

A rocking chair front porch welcomes you home to this well-planned design. The kitchen is the heart of the home, opening to the family room, breakfast area, and grand salon. A master suite on the main floor provides a relaxing retreat that opens to a terrace. The second floor boasts two additional bedrooms and a loft.

Meadowshire

GARRELL ASSOCIATES, INC.

BEDROOMS	3
BATH	2-1/2
WIDTH	78'7"
DEPTH	57'2"
1ST FLOOR	2038 sq ft
2ND FLOOR	876 sq ft
LIVING AREA	2914 sq ft
BONUS ROOM	68 sq ft
FOUNDATION	CRAWL SPACE OR BASEMENT
PLAN NUMBER	**SDHGA01-06073**

FIRST FLOOR

SECOND FLOOR

2001 Donald A. Gardner, Inc.

FIRST FLOOR

SECOND FLOOR

PRICING FOR SDHDG01-936

Sets	Price
1	$665
5	$725
8	$775
VELLUM	$1090
CD	$1980

REAR ELEVATION

Stone and siding create a stunning exterior, especially when combined with a sloped roofline and decorative wood bracket, while inside, the loft makes a perfect sitting or study area that receives a lot of light from the open, two-story great room. The second floor bathroom includes twin lavatories, and the versatile bonus room is easily accessible. Note the reach-in pantry.

Verdigre

DONALD A. GARDNER ARCHITECTS, INC.

BEDROOMS 3
BATH 2-1/2
WIDTH . . . . 59'2"
DEPTH. . . . . 44'4"
1ST FLOOR. . . . . 1547 sq ft
2ND FLOOR. . . . . 684 sq ft
LIVING AREA . . . . 2231 sq ft
BONUS ROOM. . . . . . . 300 sq ft
FOUNDATION. . . . . CRAWL SPACE*
PLAN NUMBER. **SDHDG01-936**

*Other options available. See page 175.

PRICING FOR
SDHDS01-6763

SETS	PRICE
1	N/A
6	$2012
8	N/A
VELLUM	$2012
CD	$3688

REAR ELEVATION

© The Sater Design Collection,

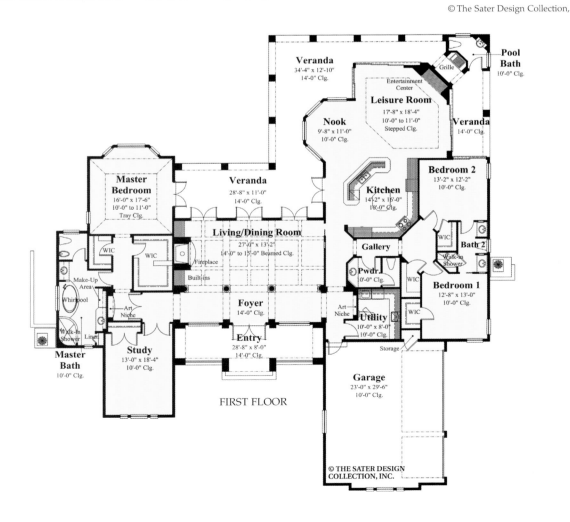

Inspired by the Southwest, this adobe home has an innovative layout. The living and dining room area enjoys a fireplace and French doors that open to the veranda. Nearby, the leisure room, nook and kitchen meld into one family-friendly area. Retreating glass walls provide a seamless connection between the common living space and the outdoors, making entertaining outside a breeze.

Shiloh

THE SATER DESIGN COLLECTION, INC.

BEDROOMS 3
BATH . . . . 2 F, 2 H
WIDTH . . . . 84'0"
DEPTH . . . . 92'0"
1ST FLOOR . . . . 3353 sq ft
LIVING AREA . . . . 3353 sq ft
FOUNDATION . . . . SLAB
PLAN NUMBER SDHDS01-6763

FIRST FLOOR

**PRICING FOR
SDHFB01-3910**

SETS	PRICE
1	$745
5	$795
8	$845
VELLUM	$995
CD	$1720

REAR ELEVATION

© 2004 Frank Betz Associates, Inc.

FIRST FLOOR

- Master Suite 14² x 17⁰ — 11'-0" HIGH CEILING
- Vaulted Family Room 17⁰ x 19⁰
- Breakfast
- Kitchen
- Vaulted M.Bath
- Foyer
- Dining Room 11⁵ x 13⁶
- Garage 20⁵ x 22⁸
- Covered Porch
- Pwdr.
- Laund.
- W.i.c.
- COPYRIGHT © 2004 FRANK BETZ ASSOCIATES, INC.

SECOND FLOOR

- Family Room Below
- Bedroom 4 13⁹ x 12⁰
- Bath
- W.i.c.
- Bedroom 3 12⁰ x 12²
- Vaulted Bedroom 2 13² x 16⁰ — 11'-0" HIGH CEILING
- Attic
- W.i.c.

The *Kensington Park's* kitchen, breakfast area and family room are all open to each other creating easy access from one area to the next. A butler's pantry connects the kitchen to the dining room for convenient entertaining. A mudroom just off the garage is equipped with a bench, wall hooks, a broom closet and access to the laundry room.

Kensington Park

FRANK BETZ
ASSOCIATES, INC.

BEDROOMS 4
BATH 3-1/2
WIDTH . . . . 56'0"
DEPTH . . . . 53'0"
1ST FLOOR . . . . 1755 sq ft
2ND FLOOR . . . . 864 sq ft
LIVING AREA . . . . 2619 sq ft
FOUNDATION . . . . CRAWL SPACE, SLAB
OR BASEMENT
PLAN NUMBER **SDHFB01-3910**

© 1996 Donald A. Gardner Architects, In

**PRICING FOR
SDHDG01-452**

SETS	PRICE
1	$780
5	$840
8	$890
VELLUM	$1235
CD	$2270

REAR ELEVATION

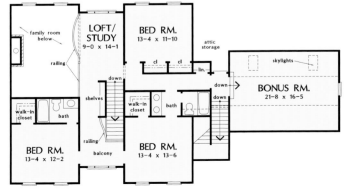

This beautiful farmhouse with twin gables and bays adds just the right amount of country style to modern family life. The master suite is tucked away downstairs with no bedrooms directly above, and the cook of the family will love the spacious kitchen with ample cabinets and pantry. Storage space abounds with walk-ins, hall shelves and a linen closet upstairs.

Arbordale

DONALD A. GARDNER ARCHITECTS, INC.

BEDROOMS 4
BATH 3-1/2
WIDTH . . . . 82'10"
DEPTH . . . . 51'8"
1ST FLOOR . . . . 2086 sq ft
2ND FLOOR . . . . 1077 sq ft
LIVING AREA . . . . 3163 sq ft
BONUS ROOM . . . . 403 sq ft
FOUNDATION . . . . CRAWL SPACE*
PLAN NUMBER **SDHDG01-452**

*Other options available. See page 175.

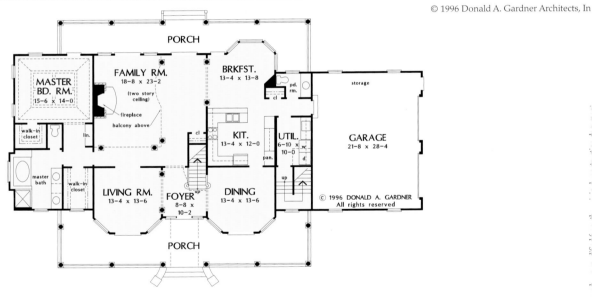

FIRST FLOOR

SECOND FLOOR

REAR ELEVATION

© The Sater Design Collection, Inc.

FIRST FLOOR

Master Suite 13'-4" x 20'-8" 10'-0" to 11'-0" Stepped Clg.

Lanai 17'-0" x 12'-11" 10'-8" Clg.

Nook 10'-0" x 11'-5" 10'-8" Clg.

Leisure Room 20'-6" x 18'-6" 10'-8" to 11'-8" Coffered Clg.

Lanai 28'-8" x 27'-0" 10'-8" Clg.

Guest Suite 13'-0" x 16'-2" 10'-0" Clg.

Guest Bath

Lanai 11'-3" x 46'-0" 10'-8" Clg.

Kitchen 18'-0" x 15'-3" 10'-8" Clg.

Living Room 11'-6" x 18'-4" 12'-4" to 13'-4" Coffered Clg.

Foyer 13'-4" Clg.

Dining 11'-8" x 14'-4" 12'-4" to 13'-4" Stepped Clg.

M. Bath 10'-0" Clg.

WIC WIC

Art Niche

Art Niche

Wet Bar

Pantry

Fireplace

WIC

Pwdr. 10'-0" Clg.

Bedroom 2 12'-0" x 12'-6" 10'-0" Clg.

Bath 2

Bedroom 3 13'-6" x 14'-10" 10'-0" Clg.

WIC

Entry 13'-4" Clg.

Utility 10'-0" Clg.

Garage 23'-0" x 32'-10" 11'-4" Clg.

© THE SATER DESIGN COLLECTION, INC.

Evocative of the adobe escapes of the Spanish Colonial vernacular, this villa integrates a graceful interior with the outdoors. Paneled doors lead to a grand foyer, which defies convention with a no-walls approach to the formal rooms. Coffered ceilings provide definition and a visual link between the private and public realms. Dramatic views further define the interior and a wraparound lanai connects public and private realms with an invitation to enjoy the outdoors.

Caprina

THE SATER DESIGN COLLECTION, INC.

BEDROOMS 4
BATH 3-1/2
WIDTH . . . . 74'8"
DEPTH. . . . . 118'0"
1ST FLOOR. . . . . 2974 sq ft
GUEST SUITE. . . . . 297 sq ft
LIVING AREA . . . . 3271 sq ft
FOUNDATION. . . . . . . SLAB
PLAN NUMBER **SDHDS01-8052**

PRICING FOR
SDHFB01-3878

SETS	PRICE
1	$745
5	$795
8	$845
VELLUM	$995
CD	$1720

REAR ELEVATION

The *Maplewood's* inviting exterior is just a taste of what's waiting inside. Transom windows along the back of the home welcome in plenty of sunshine, brightening each room. A coffered ceiling, fireplace and built-in cabinetry in the family room make for an attractive center point of the home.

Maplewood

FRANK BETZ ASSOCIATES, INC.

BEDROOMS 4
BATH 2-1/2
WIDTH . . . . 61'0"
DEPTH . . . . 70'6"
1ST FLOOR . . . . 2400 sq ft
LIVING AREA . . . . 2400 sq ft
OPT. 2ND FLOOR . . . . . 845 sq ft
FOUNDATION . . . . CRAWL SPACE, SLAB OR BASEMENT
PLAN NUMBER **SDHFB01-3878**

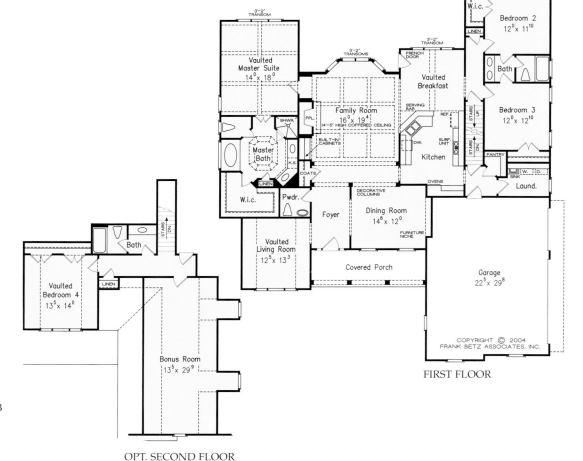

FIRST FLOOR

OPT. SECOND FLOOR

**PRICING FOR
SDHGA01-02141**

SETS	PRICE
1	N/A
5	$1495
8	N/A
VELLUM	$1595
CD	$2445

REAR ELEVATION

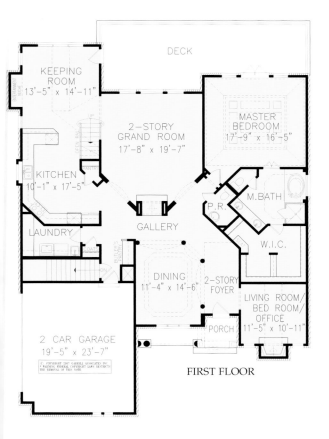

FIRST FLOOR

- KEEPING ROOM 13'-5" x 14'-11"
- DECK
- 2-STORY GRAND ROOM 17'-8" x 19'-7"
- MASTER BEDROOM 17'-9" x 16'-5"
- KITCHEN 10'-1" x 17'-5"
- M.BATH
- P.R.
- LAUNDRY
- GALLERY
- W.I.C.
- DINING 11'-4" x 14'-6"
- 2-STORY FOYER
- 2 CAR GARAGE 19'-5" x 23'-7"
- LIVING ROOM/ BED ROOM/ OFFICE 11'-5" x 10'-11"
- PORCH

SECOND FLOOR

- KITCHEN BELOW
- 2-STORY GRAND ROOM/ OPT. MEDIA ROOM
- STORAGE 8'-4" x 7'-6"
- B#2
- W.I.C.
- COMPUTER/ LOFT
- BEDROOM#2 13'-5" x 14'-2"
- WIC
- BEDROOM#3 12'-4" x 14'-11"
- 2-STORY FOYER BELOW
- B#3
- UNFINISHED/ OPT. SITTING AREA 11'-11" x 18'-9"

Perfect for a quiet retreat or a family home, the *Lynford* is reminiscent of an English cottage. Inside the plan is comfortable and dramatic with flowing yet elegant spaces. The two-sided fireplace is enjoyed from the foyer, dining and grand rooms. A first-floor master suite provides relaxation after a long day. Three additional bedrooms and a media room upstairs complete this lovely home.

Lynford

GARRELL ASSOCIATES, INC.

BEDROOMS 3
BATH 3-1/2
WIDTH . . . . 52'10"
DEPTH . . . . 67'10"
1ST FLOOR . . . . 2190 sq ft
2ND FLOOR . . . . 799 sq ft
LIVING AREA . . . . 2989 sq ft
BONUS ROOM . . . . 335 sq ft
FOUNDATION . . . . CRAWL SPACE, SLAB OR BASEMENT
PLAN NUMBER **SDHGA01-02141**

PRICING FOR SDHDS01-6787

SETS	PRICE
1	N/A
6	$2075
8	N/A
VELLUM	$2075
CD	$3804

COURTYARD VIEW

This charming courtyard home features private, family and guest spaces filled with Mediterranean design details and open connections to the loggia with fountain pool. The leisure room has a two-story boxed-beamed ceiling, a wall of built-ins, and retreating glass walls that make it one with the loggia. Nearby, the formal dining and living rooms open to a private lanai. The second-level includes a study, guest bedrooms and multiple decks with courtyard views.

Salcito

THE SATER DESIGN COLLECTION, INC.

BEDROOMS 4
BATH 4-1/2
WIDTH . . . . 45'0", 52'2" w/Garden
DEPTH . . . . 94'0"
1ST FLOOR . . . . 2087 sq ft
2ND FLOOR . . . . 1099 sq ft
GUEST ROOM . . . . 272 sq ft
LIVING AREA . . . . 3458 sq ft
FOUNDATION . . . . SLAB
PLAN NUMBER SDHDS01-6787

FIRST FLOOR

SECOND FLOOR

PRICING FOR SDHFB01-3952

SETS	PRICE
1	$870
5	$920
8	$970
VELLUM	$1190
CD	$2065

REAR ELEVATION

© 2005 Frank Betz Associates, Inc.

VAULTED BEAMED CEILING

Vaulted Master Suite
14⁰ x 18⁸

His   Hers
MIRROR

Deck

Vaulted Covered Porch
18⁹ x 14⁰

FRENCH DOOR

Breakfast

OPEN RAIL   STAIRS UP   STAIRS DN

DRYING AREA

SHWR   SEAT

Vaulted M.Bath

NICHE   PKT. DR.
LINEN

BEAMED CEILING

Vaulted Family Room
18² x 17⁰

SERVING BAR

FPL

REF   DW.

Kitchen
SURFACE UNIT

OVENS

BUILT-IN CABINETS

PANTRY
COATS

Laund.
SINK   W.   D.

Garage
21⁰ x 24⁹

Bath

Foyer

DECORATIVE COLUMNS

Dining Room
12⁰ x 13⁰

COVERED ENTRY

COPYRIGHT © 2005
FRANK BETZ ASSOCIATES, INC.

Study/ Bedrm. 4
12⁰ x 13¹⁰

Covered Porch

FIRST FLOOR

Bedroom 3
12⁰ x 12⁰

STAIRS DN

OPEN RAIL

W.i.c.   LIN   LINEN   Opt. W.i.c.

Bath   Opt. Bonus Room
16⁰ x 23⁸

DESK
K.S.

Bedroom 2
12⁶ x 15²

W.i.c.

SECOND FLOOR

The spaciousness of the *Summerlake* offers many amenities usually reserved for much larger homes. The luxurious main level master suite offers, a built-in niche, drying area and connecting his-and-her closets with a dressing mirror. An additional bedroom on the main level can be used as such or converted to a study. Upstairs, there are two additional bedrooms.

Summerlake

FRANK BETZ ASSOCIATES, INC.

BEDROOMS 4
BATH 3
WIDTH . . . . 62'4"
DEPTH . . . . 64'0"
1ST FLOOR . . . . 2145 sq ft
2ND FLOOR . . . . 754 sq ft
LIVING AREA . . . . 2899 sq ft
OPT. BONUS ROOM . . . 385 sq ft
FOUNDATION . . . . CRAWL SPACE, SLAB OR BASEMENT
PLAN NUMBER **SDHFB01-3952**

PRICING FOR SDHDG01-1009

SETS	PRICE
1	$710
5	$770
8	$820
VELLUM	$1155
CD	$2110

REAR ELEVATION

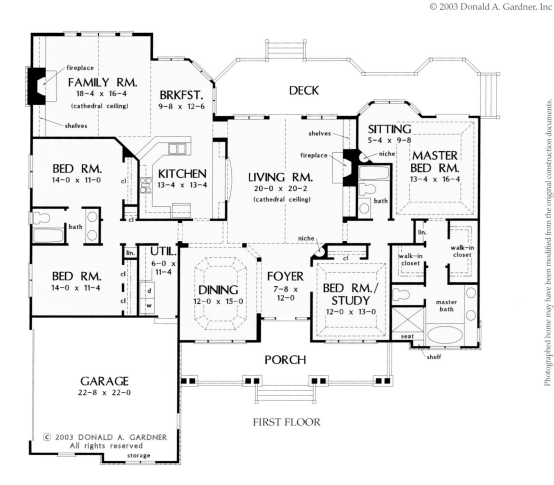

© 2003 Donald A. Gardner, Inc

Promoting easy living, this home combines Craftsman character with a low-maintenance exterior. Double-doors open into the study/bedroom, and art niches, fireplaces and built-in cabinetry add beauty and convenience. The kitchen has a well-located pass-thru to the great room, while the master suite features a bay sitting area and custom accents. A spacious deck and porch expand living outdoors.

Edgewater

DONALD A. GARDNER ARCHITECTS, INC.

BEDROOMS 4
BATH 3
WIDTH . . . . 70'0"
DEPTH. . . . . 69'10"
1ST FLOOR. . . . . 2818 sq ft
LIVING AREA . . . . 2818 sq ft
FOUNDATION. . . . . . . CRAWL SPACE*
PLAN NUMBER. **SDHDG01-1009**

*Other options available. See page 175.

FAMILY RM.
18-4 x 16-4
(cathedral ceiling)

fireplace

shelves

BRKFST.
9-8 x 12-6

DECK

SITTING
5-4 x 9-8

shelves

fireplace

niche

MASTER
BED RM.
13-4 x 16-4

BED RM.
14-0 x 11-0

KITCHEN
13-4 x 13-4

LIVING RM.
20-0 x 20-2
(cathedral ceiling)

bath

bath

cl

cl

niche

lin.

walk-in
closet

walk-in
closet

BED RM.
14-0 x 11-4

UTIL.
6-0 x 11-4

DINING
12-0 x 15-0

FOYER
7-8 x 12-0

niche

cl

BED RM./
STUDY
12-0 x 13-0

lin.

master
bath

lin.

d

w

seat

shelf

PORCH

GARAGE
22-8 x 22-0

storage

FIRST FLOOR

PRICING FOR SDHDS01-7080

SETS	PRICE
1	N/A
6	$1999
8	N/A
VELLUM	$1999
CD	$3664

REAR VIEW

The Sater Design Collection, Inc.

Solana
32'-4" x 10'-6"
10'-0" Clg.

Outdoor Grille
U.C. Ref.

Guest Suite
13'-0" x 12'-8"
10'-0" Clg.

G. Bath
10'-0" Clg.

WIC

Leisure Room
18'-0" x 22'-10"
10'-0" to 11'-0"
Stepped Clg.

Walk-In Shower WIC

Nook
10'-0" Clg.

Lanai
32'-6" x 10'-6"
10'-0" Clg.

Bedroom 2
13'-0" x 12'-6"
10'-0" Clg.

Kitchen
15'-4" x 16'-4"
10'-0" to 11'-0"
Stepped Clg.

Living Room
16'-8" x 15'-6"
12'-0" to 13'-4"
Stepped Clg.

Fireplace w/ Hearth

Built-In

Pwdr
10'-0" Clg.

Master Suite
13'-8" x 18'-5"
Stepped Clg.

Built-In

Pantry

Bath
10'-0" Clg.

M. Foyer
10'-0" Clg.

WIC

WIC

Bedroom 1
13'-6" x 12'-0"
10'-0" Clg.

Utility
8'-0" x 8'-0"
10'-0" Clg.

Dining Room
11'-2" x 12'-2"
Stepped Clg.

Foyer
10'-0" Clg.

Study
9'-10" x 13'-2"
Stepped Clg.

Built-In Bookshelves

WIC

Entry
10'-0" Clg.

M. Bath
10'-0" Clg.

Whirlpool

Walk-In Shower

Privacy Garden

©THE SATER DESIGN COLLECTION, INC.

Garage
22'-0" x 36'-2"
10'-0" Clg.

FIRST FLOOR

Hipped rooflines, twin dormers and graceful slump arches adorn this country estate. Inside, the open nature of the floor plan allows fresh breezes to move freely through the dining room to the living room, kitchen nook and leisure room— each one leading smoothly to the next past hand-crafted pillars and through elegantly arched doorways. Retreating glass doors further extend the living space outward, providing a seamless connection to the lanai.

Manchester

THE SATER DESIGN COLLECTION, INC.

BEDROOMS 4
BATH 3-1/2
WIDTH . . . . 68'8"
DEPTH. . . . . 106'0"
1ST FLOOR. . . . . 3331 sq ft
LIVING AREA . . . . 3331 sq ft
FOUNDATION. . . . . CRAWL SPACE
PLAN NUMBER. **SDHDS01-7080**

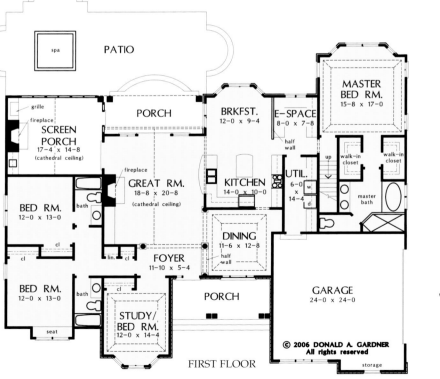

PRICING FOR SDHDG01-1180

SETS	PRICE
1	$665
5	$725
8	$775
VELLUM	$1090
CD	$1980

REAR ELEVATION

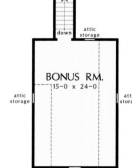

This stunning exterior commands attention from all passersby. The family-friendly interior features a spacious breakfast, kitchen and E-space area that will promote family time. Perfect for summer cookouts, the porch and patio provide a place to relax, while the screen porch with outdoor grille and fireplace allows outdoor fun in cooler climates.

Carinthia

DONALD A. GARDNER ARCHITECTS, INC.

BEDROOMS 4
BATH 3
WIDTH . . . . 73'4"
DEPTH . . . . 62'4"
1ST FLOOR . . . . 2445 sq ft
LIVING AREA . . . . 2445 sq ft
BONUS ROOM . . . . 445 sq ft
FOUNDATION . . . . CRAWL SPACE*
PLAN NUMBER **SDHDG01-1180**

*Other options available. See page 175.

FIRST FLOOR

BONUS RM.
15-0 x 24-0

PRICING FOR SDHFB01-3783

SETS	PRICE
1	$810
5	$860
8	$910
VELLUM	$1095
CD	$1895

2003 Frank Betz Associates, Inc.

REAR ELEVATION

KEEPING ROOM 13⁰ x 12⁰

Bedroom 4 11⁵ x 12⁰

Two Story Family Room 15⁰ x 19⁰

Breakfast

FPL.

FRENCH DOOR

PANTRY
ISLAND
DW.
REF.

Bath

STAIRS DN
STAIRS UP

OPEN RAIL

Kitchen

OVENS
SURFACE UNIT

COATS

NICHE

Two Story Foyer

Dining Room 12⁰ x 12⁰

Garage 20⁵ x 21⁹

Covered Porch

COPYRIGHT © 2003
FRANK BETZ ASSOCIATES, INC.

FIRST FLOOR

Sitting Room 13⁰ x 12⁰

RADIUS WINDOW

TRAY CEILING

Bedroom 3 11⁵ x 12¹⁰

Family Room Below

Master Suite 13⁵ x 17⁰

OPEN RAIL
STAIRS DN

Bath

LINEN

OVERLOOK

OPEN RAIL

RADIUS WINDOW

Foyer Below

Bedroom 2 12⁰ x 12⁰

W.
Laund.

Vaulted M.Bath

LINEN

SHWR.

LINEN

W.i.c.

SECOND FLOOR

The Craftsman-style home has made a comeback! Tapered columns and Mission-styled windows, combined with earthen stone and cedar shakes, makes the *Bakersfield* reminiscent of the Craftsman era. Relaxing family time is well spent in the keeping room just off the kitchen. Tray ceilings and a private lounging area make the master suite a true retreat.

Bakersfield

FRANK BETZ ASSOCIATES, INC.

BEDROOMS 4
BATH 3
WIDTH . . . . 48'0"
DEPTH . . . . 50'0"
1ST FLOOR . . . . 1322 sq ft
2ND FLOOR . . . . 1262 sq ft
LIVING AREA . . . . 2584 sq ft
FOUNDATION . . . . CRAWL SPACE, SLAB OR BASEMENT
PLAN NUMBER **SDHFB01-3783**

Before You Order

QUICK TURNAROUND
Because you're placing your order directly with the designer, plans can be shipped quickly. Orders placed before noon ET will typically ship the same day. Some restrictions may apply. Plans cannot be shipped to a PO Box; please provide a street address.

EXCHANGE POLICY
Since sets are printed at the time you place your order, returns are not acceptable. If you find that the plan you purchased does not meet your needs, you may exchange it for another plan in the same designer's collection within 60 days of the original purchase. Exchanges incur a processing fee of 20% of the total amount of the original order plus the difference in price between the plans (if applicable) and the cost to ship new plans to you. Vellums and plans on CD cannot be exchanged. All sets must be returned and authorization given before the exchange can take place. Please call 1-866-525-9374 if you have any questions.

LOCAL BUILDING CODES AND ZONING REQUIREMENTS
The plans in this magazine are designed, at the time of creation, to meet or exceed national building standards. Because of differences in geography and climate, each state, county and municipality has its own building codes and zoning requirements. Your plan may need to be modified to comply with the local codes and requirements. Prior to using your plans, the designers strongly advise that you consult a local building official.

ARCHITECTURE AND ENGINEERING SEALS
Due to concern over energy costs, safety, structural integrity and other factors, some cities and states are now requiring that a licensed architect or engineer review and approve any set of building documents prior to permit application or start of actual construction. The designers strongly advise that you consult your local building official to see if such a review is required.

DISCLAIMER
Each designer has put substantial care and effort into the creation of these plans. The designers authorize the use of their plans on the express condition that you strictly comply with all local building codes, zoning requirements and other applicable laws, regulations, and ordinances. Because the designers cannot provide on-site consultation, supervision or control over actual construction, and because of the great variance in local building requirements, practices and soil, seismic, weather and other conditions, THE DESIGNERS CANNOT MAKE ANY WARRANTY, EXPRESS OR IMPLIED, WITH RESPECT TO THE CONTENT OR USE OF THEIR PRINTS OR VELLUMS, INCLUDING BUT NOT LIMITED TO ANY WARRANTY OF MERCHANTABILITY OR OF FITNESS FOR A PARTICULAR PURPOSE.

IGNORING COPYRIGHT LAWS CAN BE A $1,000,000 MISTAKE!
US copyright laws allow for statutory penalties up to $150,000 per incident for copyright infringement involving any of the copyrighted plans found in this publication. The law can be confusing. So, for your own protection, take the time to understand what you cannot do when it comes to home plans.

WHAT YOU CAN'T DO!
- You cannot duplicate home plans.
- You cannot copy any part of a home plan to create another
- You cannot build a home without purchasing a set with a license to build. Study sets do not include licenses.

Plan Checklist

HOW MANY SETS DO YOU NEED?

_____ **OWNER**
(one set for notes, one for file)

_____ **BUILDER**
(generally requires at least three sets; one as a legal document, one for inspections and at least one to give subcontractors)

_____ **LOCAL BUILDING DEPARTMENT**
(often requires two sets)

_____ **MORTGAGE LENDER**
(usually one set for a conventional loan; three sets for FHA or VA loans)

_____ **TOTAL NUMBER OF SETS**

Most designers offer single plan sets so that you may study and plan your dream home in detail; however, you cannot use them to build. Single sets are stamped "NOT FOR CONSTRUCTION." If you are planning to get cost estimates or wish to begin building immediately you will need more sets. Because extra sets are less expensive when purchased together, make sure you order enough to satisfy your needs. The checklist on the left will help you determine the number of sets you will need. If changes are needed, we recommend ordering reproducible vellums so changes can be made directly to the plan. Vellums are the only set that can be reproduced; it is illegal to copy blueprints.

Additional Items†

Blueprints (per set) $60.00

Full Reverse Blueprints* $145.00

MATERIALS LIST $80.00

BASEMENT PLANS* .... From $225-$275.00

(no charge for Frank Betz plans)

*Call for availability and pricing for your plan.

SHIPPING & HANDLING

Based on one plan package being shipped.
Higher rates may apply if multiple plan packages are shipped.

Overnight $45.00

Priority Overnight $55.00

2nd Day $35.00

Ground $22.00

Saturday (if available) $55.00

International Delivery ... (Please call for prices & availability.)

†Products and prices vary for each designer.
Call for specific availability and pricing.

Price Worksheet
Refer to prices on each plan page.

PLAN   **NUMBER**

☐ 1 set (study only) ....$_____

☐ 5-set building package ....$_____

☐ 8-set building package ....$_____

☐ 1 set of reproducible vellums ....$_____

☐ CD or Electronic File ....$_____

_____ Additional Identical Plans @ $60 each ......$_____

FOUNDATION OPTIONS:

_____ Full Reverse Plans @ $145 each ....$_____

_____ Crawl Space_____ Slab_____ Basement......$_____
(no charge for Frank Betz plans)

SUB TOTAL $_____

SHIPPING AND HANDLING $_____

SALES TAX (Will be determined upon placing order) $_____

TOTAL $_____

TO ORDER CALL: 1-866-525-9374

WWW.SMALLDREAMHOMES.COM

To Order a Plan or for More Information:
CALL TOLL-FREE
1-866-525-9374

PLEASE NOTE THE DESIGNER OF YOUR CHOSEN PLAN BEFORE CALLING. FOLLOW THE MENU PROMPTS TO MAKE DIRECT CONTACT WITH THE DESIGNERS OFFICE.

MANY PLANS CAN BE MODIFIED TO SUIT YOUR NEEDS OFTEN BY THE ORIGINAL DESIGN FIRM.

FOR MORE INFORMATION ABOUT

PLAN MODIFICATION PLEASE VISIT:

WWW.SMALLDREAMHOMES.COM

Plan Index